Quatrains

TRÜBNER'S

ORIENTAL SERIES

THE QUATRAINS

OF

OMAR KHAYYÁM

*THE PERSIAN TEXT WITH AN ENGLISH VERSE
TRANSLATION*

BY

E H WHINFIELD, M.A
LATE OF THE BENGAL CIVIL SERVICE

Second Edition, Corrected and Enlarged

LONDON
KEGAN PAUL, TRENCH, TRÜBNER & CO, Limited
Paternoster House
Charing Cross Road, W C
1901
[All rights reserved]

LONDON
GILBERT AND RIVINGTON, LIMITED
ST JOHN'S HOUSE, CLERKENWELL

"Akbar expressed the opinion that after every ode of Háfiz one ought to write a quatrain of Omar Khayyám, otherwise reading the ode is like wine without a relish (*ga áh*)"—*Ain i Akbari* Blochmann's edition, vol. ii., p 238

INTRODUCTION

——◆——

§ 1.

The Life of Omar.

GHIÁS uddín Abul Fath Omar bin Ibrahím al Khayyám was born early in the 5th century A.H. in the
province of Khorásan, and lived during the greater
part of his life at Nishapúr, one of the chief cities of
that province, where he died in 517 A H Khorásan
was wrested from the Ghaznavides by Toghrul Beg, the
chief of the Seljuk Turks, in 431 A H., and formed the
nucleus of the empire which was extended by Toghrul
and his successors, Alp Arslan and Malik Shah, to the
shores of the Mediterranean before the end of that
century. The whole story may be read in Gibbon's
57th chapter, but it has little bearing on the subject of
the present notice. Omar was as sublimely indifferent
to the stirring events of his time as Goethe at Jena
With the exception of a panegyric on Malik Shah and
a possible allusion to the murder of Nizám ul Mulk,
his quatrains contain no references whatever to the
affairs of the time. The Turks were occupied in

making fresh conquests, and seem to have left the
conquered Persians of Khorásan pretty well to themselves, in fact, during the reigns of Alp Arslan and
Malik Shah, the internal government of the conquered
provinces was in the hands of a native Persian, the
great Wazir Nizám ul Mulk, who was especially
inclined to favour learned men like Omar. Whether
Nizám ul Mulk was his fellow-student and afterwards
his special patron is not certain. It is unnecessary to
repeat the well-known story of the three school-
companions, recorded in the *Wasáyá* or *Nasáyih*,
attributed to Nizám ul Mulk It now turns out that
this work was not written by him but by one of his
descendants in the 9th century A.H.* The earliest book
in which this story occurs is the *Jami' ut Tawáríkh* of
the unfortunate Rashíd ud Din, who was put to death
in 718 A.H.† The difficulties in the way of accepting it
are (1) the chronological one, as I pointed out in my first
(1883) edition Nizám ul Mulk was born in 408 A.H.‡
and murdered in 485 A.H. at the age of seventy-seven,
while Omar and Hasan lived till the years 517 A.H.
and 518 A.H. respectively It seems improbable that
both of them should have lived to such extreme old age
(2) The fact that Omar, in the preface to his Algebra,§

---

* See Rieu's Catalogue, vol. ii, p 446

† See Mr. E G Browne's paper in Journal R A S, vol 31,
p 409

‡ This date is assigned as that of Nizám ul Mulk's birth by
Abul Faraj and Ibn Khalhkán (See Vullers, "Geschichte der
Seldschuken," p 107, note and Journal R. A S, vol 31, p 415)

§ See Woepcke, "L Algèbre d Omar Alkhayyámí," p 4

mentions one Abu Táhir as his patron, and not
Nizám ul Mulk; but the Algebra may have been
written after Nizám ul Mulk's murder, and when Omar
had found another patron   (3) The fact that Omar's
contemporary, Nizámi i 'Arúzí, in his notice of Omar,
makes no mention of the story. Professor Houtsma, in
his edition of Bondari's "History of the Seljuks,"
suggests that it may have arisen from a confusion
between Nizám ul Mulk and the Wazir Anushirwan
ibn Khalid, who left memoirs covering the years
466 A.H —528 A.H., in which he states he had been at
school with Hasan i Sabbah. Mr. H. Beveridge has
discussed the evidence for the story very fully, but
though desirous to support it, he admits that the
chronology is a difficulty.*

In 467 A H., according to Ibn ul Athir and Abu l
Feda, Omar was appointed chief astronomer, and he
held this office till the death of Malik Shah in
485 A.H. He was, therefore, in all probability, middle-
aged in 467 A H. During his tenure of this office
he compiled the astronomical tables known as *Zij
i Malikshahi*,† and, in conjunction with seven other
astronomers, he reformed the old Persian calendar
named the Era of Yazdajird. An account of this
reform is given by Mahmud Shah Khulji, which
will be found in the Appendix, Note C. The reform
mainly consisted in a more exact ascertainment of
the length of the solar year, and in an improved

---

* Journal R. A. S., vol 31, p. 135.
† Haji Khalfa, vol. iii , p 570.

system of intercalation which, according to Reinaud,[*] is preferred by some astronomers to that adopted by Pope Gregory XIII five centuries later. The reformed calendar did not, however, displace the Hijra (lunar) era in common use

Omar was also highly distinguished as a mathematician. A work of his on Algebra has been edited and translated by M. Woepcke of Bonn, and another. "On the Difficulties of Euclid's Definitions," is preserved in the Leyden Library. His work on Algebra enjoyed a high reputation for several centuries Ibn Khaldún refers to it in his Prolegomena, and Haji Khalfa quotes the commencement. M. Woepcke praises him for his power of generalization and his rigorously systematic procedure

The following anecdotes of Omar are found in the *Chahár Maqála* of Nizámi i 'Arúzí of Samarkand, which was written about the middle of the 6th century A H. I quote from Mr. E G Browne's translation in the Journal R. A. S.[†] —

(1) "In the year A.H. 506. Khwája Imám Omar Khayyam and Khwája Imám Muzaffar-i-Isfizárí had alighted in the city of Balkh, in the Street of the Slave-sellers, in the house of Amir Abú Sa'd, and I had joined that assembly. In the midst of our convivial gathering I heard that Argument of Truth, Omar, say, 'My grave will be in a spot where the trees will shed their blossoms on me twice in each year.' This thing

---

seemed to me impossible, though I knew that one such
as he would not speak idle words

"When I arrived at Nishapúr in the year A.H. 530, it
being then some years since that great man had veiled
his countenance in the dust, and this lower world had
been bereaved of him, I went to visit his grave on the
eve of a Friday (seeing that he had the claim of a
master on me) taking with me a guide to point out to
me his tomb So he brought me out to the Híra
Cemetery. I turned to the left, and his tomb lay at the
foot of a garden-wall, over which pear-trees and peach-
trees thrust their heads, and on his grave had fallen so
many flower-leaves that his dust was hidden beneath
the flowers. Then I remembered that saying which I
had heard from him in the city of Balkh, and I fell to
weeping, because on the face of the earth, and in all the
regions of the habitable globe, I nowhere saw one like
unto him May God (blessed and exalted is He) have
mercy upon him, by His Grace and His Favour! Yet
although I witnessed this prognostication on the part
of that Proof of the Truth, Omar, I did not observe that
he had any great belief in astrological predictions , nor
have I seen or heard of any of the great [scientists]
who had such belief."*

(2) "In the winter of the year A.H. 508 the King †
sent a messenger to Merv to the Prime Minister Sadru 'd-

---

* I quoted the above story in my first edition from the
version given in the preface to the Calcutta edition of the
Rubá'iyát

† This was Muhammad, second son of Malik Shah, who
reigned from 498—511 A.H. (see Vullers).

Din Muhammad b. al-Muzaffar (on whom be God's
Mercy) bidding him tell Khwája Imám Omar to select
a favourable time for him to go hunting, such that
therein should be no snowy or rainy days ; for Khwája
Imám Omar was in the Minister's company, and used to
lodge at his house

" So the Minister sent a messenger to summon him,
and told him what had happened. The Khwája went
and looked into the matter for two days and made a
careful choice ; and he himself went and superintended
the mounting of the King at the auspicious moment.
When the King was mounted and had gone but a short
distance, the sky became overcast with clouds, a wind
arose, and snow and mist supervened. All present fell
to laughing, and the King desired to turn back ; but
Khwája Imám [Omar] said, 'Have no anxiety, for
this very hour the clouds will clear away, and during
these five days there will be not a drop of moisture.'
So the King rode on, and the clouds opened, and during
those five days there was no moisture, and no one saw
a cloud.

" But prognostication by the stars, though a recognized
art, is not to be relied on, and whatever the astrologer
predicts he must leave to Fate."

These two anecdotes are important because they are
related by one who knew Omar personally, and who, be
it remarked, had a great respect for him.

The next notice of Omar is contained in the *Nuzhat
ul-Arwáh*** by Muhammad Shahrazuri, who wrote about

---

* Haji Khalfa mentions this book, but does not give its date
(vol. vi., p. 321)

650 A.H. I quote from the translation of Professor Denison Ross in the Journal R. A S.*:—

"Omar Al-Khayyámí was a Nishapuri by birth and extraction. He [may be regarded as] the successor of Abú 'Ali (Avicena) in the various branches of philosophic learning; but he was a man of bad character, and disliked entertaining. While he was in Ispahan he perused a certain book seven times, and then knew it by heart. On his return to Nishapur he dictated it [from memory], and on comparing this with the original copy, it was found that the difference between them was but slight. He was averse both to composition and to teaching. He is the author of a handbook on natural science, and of two pamphlets, one entitled *Al-Wujúd*, and the other *Al-Kawn wa't Taklíf.* He was learned in the law, in classical Arabic, and in history.

"One day Al-Khayyám went to see the Wazír 'Abd-ur-Razzák. The chief of the Korán Readers, Abú-l-Hasan Al-Ghazzálí, was with this latter [at the time], and the two were discussing the disagreement of the Korán Readers in regard to a certain verse. [As Omar entered] the Wazír said, 'Here we have *the* authority,' and proceeded to ask Al-Khayyámí [for his opinion] on the matter. [Omar] enumerated the various readings of the Readers, and explained the grounds for each one. He also mentioned the exceptional readings and the

* Vol 30, p 352. Mr. H Beveridge (Journal R A. S., vol 32, p 550) has proved that this work is the one wrongly described by Cureton as the Tarikh ul Hukama of Shahristani, mentioned by Haji Khalfa (ii, p 125) See Cureton's edition of Shahristani's "Book of Sects," p. ii, note e.

arguments in favour of each, and expressed his
preference for one view in particular

"Al-Ghazzáli then said, 'May God add such men as
thee to the number of the learned! Of a truth I did
not think any one of the Korán Readers knew the
readings by heart to this extent—much less one of
the [secular] philosophers'

"As for the sciences, he had mastered both mathematics and philosophy. One day the 'Proof of Islám,'
Al-Ghazzáli,* came to see him, and asked him how it
came that one could distinguish one of the parts of the
sphere, which revolves on the axis, from the rest,
although the sphere was similar in all its parts Al-
Khayyámí pronounced his views, beginning with a
certain category, but he refrained from entering deeply
into discussion—and such was the wont of this respected
Sheykh [Their conversation was interrupted by] the
call to mid-day prayer, whereupon Al-Ghazzáli said,
'Truth has come in, and lying has gone out.' Omar
arose and went to visit Sultan Sanjar. The latter was
[at the time] a mere child,† and was suffering from an
attack of small-pox. When he came away the Wazir
asked him, 'How did you find the child, and what did
you prescribe for him?' Omar answered, 'The child

---

* This was the celebrated Abu Hamíd ul Ghazzáh, the Schel-
ling of Moslem philosophy, and author of the *Ihya 'l'lúm ud-
Hin*, born at Tús in 450 A H, and died there in 505 A.H (Ibu
Khalhkán, vol. ii., p. 621)

† Sanjar was born in 479 A H, being the third son of Malik
Shah, and reigned from 511—552, in which year he died. (See
Vullers, "Mirchond's Geschichte der Seldschuken," p 171.)

is in a most precarious state.' An Ethiopian slave reported this saying to the Sultan, and when the Sultan recovered he became inimical to Omar, and did not like him Malik-shah treated him as a boon companion , and Shams-ul-Mulk honoured him greatly, and made him sit beside him on his throne.

" It is related that [Omar] was [one day] picking his teeth with a toothpick of gold, and was studying the chapter on Metaphysics from [Avicena's] 'Book of Healing.' When he reached the section on 'The One and the Many' he placed the toothpick between the two leaves, arose, performed his prayers, and made his last injunctions. He neither ate nor drank anything [that day], and when he performed the last evening prayer, he bowed himself to the ground, and said as he bowed, 'O God ! verily I have known Thee to the extent of my power: forgive me therefore. Verily my knowledge of Thee is my recommendation to Thee.' And [so saying] he died. may God have pity on him !

"He wrote beautiful verses both in Arabic and in Persian, of which the following may serve as examples "

Here follow in the article three short Arabic kasídas, in the place of which, however, the Persian translation quotes two Persian quatrains, namely Nos. 193 and 230, infra.

Another notice of Omar, of a very uncomplimentary kind, occurs in the Mirsad ul-'Ibád, a Sufi treatise written in 620 A H. by Nejm ud-Din Razi, a friend of Jaláluddin Rumi.* I quote from Professor Denison

---

* See Rieu's Catalogue, p 38

Ross' translation in the Journal R. A. S.* After detailing the blessings secured by piety, &c, he proceeds:—

"But those unfortunate philosophers and materialists who are shut out from both these blessings are bewildered and have gone astray with a certain man of letters, who is famous among them for his talent, his wisdom, his sagacity, and his learning. And that man is Omar Khayyám. To form an estimate of his utter shamelessness and corruption, it is only necessary to read the following verses composed by him."

Here follow the quatrains Nos 508 and 126 in my text. This passage is important as showing that the stricter Sufis by no means held his poems in such esteem as some are represented in the next notice to have done.

This notice is that contained in the Tarikh ul Hukama of Ibn al Qitti (? Qibti), who died in 646 A.H. The passage was cited by Woepcke in his "L'Algèbre d'Omar Alkhayyami," and translated by me in my first edition. Professor Schukovski has collated Woepcke's text with the MSS of Berlin, Munich and Vienna, and Professor Denison Ross has given a translation of this corrected text in the Journal R. A. S.† from which I quote —

"Omar Al-Khayyám, Imám of Khorasan, and the most learned man of his day, was versed in the science of the Greeks. He encouraged the search after the One Judge, by means of the purification of the inclinations of the flesh for the sake of the elevation of the

---

human soul. He pointed out the necessity of studying
political science according to the principles of the
Greeks. The later Sufis have found themselves in
agreement with some of the exterior meanings of his
verses, and have introduced them into their system, and
discuss them in their public and private gatherings
But their inner meaning is a stinging serpent to the
Shari'a . . .

"But since the people of his day reviled him for his
religion, and exposed to view the secrets he had veiled
from them, he feared for his blood, and reined the
bridle of his tongue and pen He performed the
Pilgrimage, not out of piety, but from fear [of men],
and revealed a secret from among his impure secrets
When he came to Baghdad men of his way of thinking
in the ancient science beset him, but he shut on them
his door, with the shutting of repentance and not of
companionship. And when he returned from the
Pilgrimage to his town, he used to go morning and
evening to the place of worship, and concealed his
secret thoughts, which, however, perforce revealed
themselves. He was without an equal in the sciences
of astronomy and philosophy, and he became proverbial
in these branches. If only he could have safeguarded
his good name!

"By him there are fugitive verses whose hidden
meaning penetrates their veil of concealment, and
whose fount of conception is troubled by the turbidness
of their secret intent."

Qazwini, who died in 677 A.H, mentions Omar in
his geographical work called *Athár ul Bilád*. The

passage is thus translated by Professor Ross in the Journal R. A. S * —

"Among the learned men of Nishapur was Omar Khayyam   He was a man versed in all branches of philosophy, especially in mathematics.   He lived in the reign of Malik Shah the Seljuk, who gave him much money for the purchase of astronomical apparatus that he might make observations of the stars, but the Sultan died ere these observations had been carried out. They relate that Omar. while staying in a certain rabat (inn), noticed that the inhabitants complained of the abundance of the birds, whose pollutions defiled their clothes. He thereupon made a bird out of clay and placed it on the highest point of the building. [After this] the birds kept away from this rabat.   It is also related that one of the doctors of the law used to come daily before sunrise to read philosophy under him, but used to denounce him to the people   So Omar called to his house all the drummers and trumpeters, and when the doctor of the law came as usual for his lesson, Omar ordered the men to beat their drums and blow their trumpets, and thus collected round himself people from every quarter.   He then addressed them, saying, 'Men of Nishapur, here is your teacher   He comes every day at this hour to me, and studies science with me, but to you he speaks of me in the manner you know.   If I am really as he says, then why does he come and study with me? and if not, why does he abuse his teacher?'"

* Vol. 30, p. 355

The *Firdaws ut Tawarikh*, written in 808 A.H., contains another but unimportant notice of Omar, and gives the quatrains Nos. 501 and 503 of my text.*

The *Tarikh i Alfi*, written by order of Akbar at the end of the 10th century A.H, repeats some of the stories about Omar already given, and gives the quatrain about the donkey.†

Ibn ul Athír, in his chronicle, which comes down to the year 628 A.H. (two years before the author's death), mentions the occurrence of a fierce religious civil war in Nishapúr in the year 489 A H during the troubles which followed the death of Malik Shah. The orthodox, under the leadership of the chiefs of the Hanefites and the Shafeites, fought against the Kerrámians or Anthropomorphist heretics, and succeeded in putting many of them to death and in destroying all their establishments ‡ Evidently Nishapúr was not a pleasant place of residence for anyone whose orthodoxy was at all doubtful.

The geographer translated by Sir. W. Ouseley, whom he supposed to be Ibn Haukal, but who was really Al-Istakhri,§ says of Nishapúr. "The city is watered by a subterranean canal, which is conveyed to the fields and

---

* Journal R A. S., vol 30, p 356 This passage was discovered by Professor Schukovski, like those above given of Shahrazuri and Razi

† My No 423. See Journal R A S., vol. 30, p 358, and Mr Beveridge's note, Journal R A. S, vol 31, p 135

‡ See Defrémery, "Recherches sur le règne de Barkiárok," p. 51

§ See Rieu's Catalogue, p. 416.

gardens, and there is a considerable stream that waters the city and the villages about it this stream is called *Saba*. In all the province of Khorasan there is not any city larger than Nishapur, nor any blessed with a more pure and temperate air "

If Omar's human surroundings were not all that he could desire, nature seems to have been pleasant enough

It is needless to give the references to Omar in Mirkhwand, the *Dabistan*, &c , as they only repeat the statements of earlier authors.

§ 2

The Text.

THE great difficulty in the way of arriving at a satisfactory text of Omar's poems arises from the exceeding variety and discrepancy of the materials. We look in vain for anything approaching to a *Textus Receptus*. The oldest MS. we possess is the Bodleian MS., written at Shiráz in 865 A H., which contains only 158 quatrains. The two Paris MSS., which, as M Fagnan told me, are both of the 10th century A H., contain 175 and 213 respectively. The MSS of later date exhibit an ever-increasing number of quatrains. the Cambridge copy, which is probably not more than 130 years old, having no less than 801, the Bombay Lithograph of 1880, 756 ; and the Lucknow Lithograph of 1894, 770.   The late Mrs. Cadell,* writing to me in November, 1882, said, "Before 1878 1 had gathered and compared from twelve MSS and M. Nicolas' edition about 1050 quatrains going about under Khayyám's name, to which I have since added perhaps 100—150 more, making together pretty nearly all the material attainable in Europe " However, in an article in *Frazer* for May, 1879, she expressed the opinion that the number of genuine quatrains is not more than 250 or 300, and I am inclined to think this estimate high enough.

The state of the case is this : Out of all the quatrains passing under Omar's name, hardly any stand alone Almost every one belongs to a family, more or less numerous, to the other members of which it bears a strong family likeness.   One can say with some confidence that all these replicas, paraphrases and variations of the same ideas can hardly be the work of one and the same man, least of all of a man of Omar's mental calibre It seems to me that no one but a mere driveller, labouring under a chronic flux of words, could possibly have said the same thing so many times over.   These are my grounds for holding that the majority of the quatrains ascribed to Omar in the later MSS. are wrongly ascribed to him, and for concurring with Mrs Cadell's opinion that the number of the genuine quatrains is not more than about 300.

---

* 144 quatrains translated by her have recently been published by Dr R Garnett (John Lane, 1899) Her son, Major Cadell, R A , tells me her Persian papers have not all been preserved

Then the question arises how to distinguish between the genuine and the spurious quatrains. The character of the language might be supposed to furnish some criterion whereby to distinguish the work of Omar from that of other poets writing long after him, but the fact is that, as remarked by Chodzko,* the literary Persian of to-day differs singularly little from that in use 800 years ago. Moreover, the archaisms in old poets are constantly being modernized by the copyists of the MSS. Again, some suppose that there is something peculiar in the subject-matter of Omar's poetry which serves to differentiate it from that of other poets. But this is quite a mistake. The poetry of revolt is supposed to be peculiar to him, but Avicena wrote in this strain before him, and Afzal Káshi and many others imitated him later on.

In this difficulty the rule I follow is to give the best specimens of each class of quatrains, and to exclude the rest. In accordance with this rule, I exclude, in particular, a large number of quatrains in praise of wine, and exhortations to live for the day, which recur in the MSS with most wearisome frequency. I have not, however, excluded any quatrains simply on account of their being ascribed to other writers as well as Omar. So long as I find fair MS. authority for such quatrains, I include them in the text, not because I am sure Omar wrote them, but because it is just as likely

* See Chodzko, "Grammaire de la Langue Persane," préface, p. xiii.

they were written by him as by the other claimants.
Of course, a text formed on these principles cannot be a
very satisfactory one, but, on the other hand, it is
useless for an editor to pretend to greater certainty
than the case admits of.

Professor Schukovski of St. Petersburg, in a recent
paper which has been translated by Professor Denison
Ross,* has attempted to identify the genuine quatrains
of Omar. His principle is that the parentage of each
quatrain must be decided by the date of the MS. in
which it first appears, e g. if a quatrain be found in
the Bodleian MS. of 865 A H , any attribution of the
same quatrain to other authors in MSS. of later date
must be regarded as erroneous. On this principle he
has ear-marked 82, which he calls "wandering"
quatrains, i e. quatrains which have wandered from
their rightful author Omar into the Diwáns of other
poets Always subject to the considerations stated on
p xxi., I think his principle a sound one, though it
must be borne in mind that a MS. of later date may
possibly preserve the contents of another MS. older
than any now extant. If I understand Professor Ross'
paper rightly, it seems doubtful if Schukovski has
always applied his principle consistently. Thus, for
instance, of the 82 "wandering" quatrains specified by
him, he seems to ascribe six to Omar on the sole
authority of Nicolas, though Nicolas nowhere names
the MSS. from which he framed his text. Again, the

---

* See Journal R A S , vol 30, p 349

quatrains 420 and 406 in my text, which Dr. Ethé[*] found attributed to Avicena and Abu Sa'id respectively, the former in eight *Tazkiras* and the latter in Elliot,[†] are ascribed to Omar by Schukovski, though only found by me in Nicolas, the Lucknow Lithograph, and two rather late MSS The weight of evidence seems to be in favour of Avicena's authorship of No. 420, whatever may be thought as to No. 406

The text has been framed from a comparison of the following authorities:—

I. The Bodleian MS., No 140 of the Ouseley Collection, containing 158 quatrains.

II The Calcutta Asiatic Society's MS, No. 1513, containing 516 quatrains

III. The India Office MS., No. 2420, ff. 212 to 267, containing 512 quatrains

IV The India Office MS., No 2486, ff. 158 to 194, containing 362 quatrains.

V The Calcutta edition of 1252 A H , containing 438 quatrains, with an appendix of 54 more, which the editor says he found in a *Bayáz*, or commonplace-book, after the others had been printed.

VI. The Paris edition of M. Nicolas, containing 464 quatrains

VII. The Lucknow lithographed edition of 1878, containing 763 quatrains.

---

* See Ethé, "Nachrichten von der Gottinger Akademie,' 1875, N S 21, p 555, and "Sitzungsberichte der Bayerischer Akademie," 1875, p. 53.

† The latter is also found in the Bengal Asiatic Society's MS of Abu Sa'id's Rubá'iyat

VIII. A fragment of an edition begun by the late Mr Blochmann, containing only 62 quatrains.

I have also consulted the Cambridge MS., for the purpose of settling one or two readings, but have not collated it throughout.

I have not given the various readings, except in cases of special importance.

I have made a point of marking the *izáfat* wherever it occurs. "The omission of this," says Lumsden, "is undoubtedly a great defect in Persian writing, insomuch that I am not certain whether it has not been the cause of more obscurity than would result from the omission of all the prepositions."*

I have also marked all the poetical contractions, *taskin*, and noted all peculiarities of metre and scansion The scanning sometimes shows where a MS. reading is wrong, sometimes determines the exact words of the text, and often furnishes the only means of detecting the presence of an *izáfat* †

§ 3.

The Translation.

ACCORDING to the tradition, the Prophet declared that it was the business of a messenger to deliver his message exactly. But when the message is in an unknown tongue, and has to be interpreted as well as

---

* See Lumsden's Persian Grammar (Calcutta, 1810), vol. ii, p 232

† See Appendix, note A

repeated, the scope of the messenger's duty is perforce somewhat enlarged. If he simply repeats the message word for word in the language of his hearers, retaining the foreign idioms and construction of the sentences, this overstraining after faithfulness only results in making the message unintelligible. A man who professes to translate into English must write English. Consequently, even when he is translating plain prose, he must allow himself such latitude as is involved in substituting English equivalents for foreign idioms and constructions.

Again, in the case of epigrammatic and lyric poetry like Omar's, where nearly the whole attractiveness lies in the style and the manner, the point and the "curious felicity" of the expression, the translator must claim still further latitude* if he wishes to convey to the reader any adequate idea of the charm of the original. Many of Omar's little "conceits," if reproduced word for word, seem absurd, some of his most felicitous expressions sound quite the reverse in English, and even his peculiar grotesque humour loses its savour. In fact, the very beauties of his style, when reproduced in bald English prose, seem uncouth and displeasing. If his poems be translated in literal prose we get the letter indeed, but it is a dead letter, from which the life and spirit have evaporated. These considerations obviously point to the adoption of verse as the best vehicle for representing Omar to English readers, and

---

* Such wider latitude is taken by the best translators of Horace's Odes, e g Conington and Martin.

of course the trammels of metre and rhyme of themselves force the translator to take still further liberties. If he does not take such liberties, no translator can convey to his readers any adequate notion of the original; indeed, it may be said that otherwise he will give a totally erroneous notion of the original

Shall we say then that a translator may take unlimited license to paraphrase? By no means. The test of the legitimacy of a paraphrase is to be found in the object with which such paraphrase is made If it be made in order to bring out the meaning and the charm of the original, it is legitimate, as in that case the translator is only trying to acquit himself of his proper duty. If, on the other hand, it be made with the object of altering the meaning to give it a modern flavour, to elevate what seems a too grovelling sentiment, or to trick out an ancient commonplace with present-day trappings, the paraphrase is unwarranted and illegitimate. It is not a translator's business to "paint the lily" He ought to present it in all its natural colouring as far as he can. These remarks are not intended to apply to Fitz-Gerald, but only to ordinary translators. Fitz-Gerald was a born poet, and the great liberties he took with Omar have been amply justified by the result.* But the ordinary translator must not venture beyond his tether.

---

* In his careful edition of the Bodleian MS, Mr. Heron Allen has rendered Fitz-Gerald the same service (or disservice?) which Ruskin rendered to Turner, viz. he has explored the sources of Fitz-Gerald's inspiration, and shown exactly how far he departed from them.

I believe these to be the main principles on which a translation of Omar ought to be made, but it is easier to lay down principles than to carry them out, even to one's own satisfaction.

As regards metre, Professor Conington laid down the rule that there should always be some degree of conformity between the metre of the original and that of the translation. The arrangement of the rhymes in the Ruba'i may be reproduced in English verse without giving undue offence to ordinary ears, indeed, some people find it rather agreeable. But as regards the length and structure of the line, there is a difficulty The normal Ruba'i line consists of 13 syllables, 7 long and 6 short, reducible by contraction to 10 syllables, all long.* The rhythm is therefore slow and protracted, and perhaps Alexandrines would be the nearest English equivalent. But few men can write tolerable Alexandrines, and an inferior workman had better not attempt them. Consequently, the translator is thrown back on the English decasyllable line, in other words, he must follow Fitz-Gerald. Of course, one who ventures to write in the metre which Fitz-Gerald has used with such success, cannot help feeling at almost every step that he is provoking comparisons very much to his own disadvantage. But I do not think this consideration ought to deter him from using the metre which seems most appropriate. The shorter length of the decasyllable line, as compared with the Persian, is not altogether a disadvantage to the translator. Owing to

---

* See Appendix, note B.

the large number of monosyllables in English, it is
generally adequate to hold the contents of a Persian
line a syllable or two longer; and a line erring, if at all,
on the side of brevity has at any rate the advantage
of obliging the translator to eschew modern diffuseness,
and of making him try to copy the "classical parci-
mony" of the original.

§ 4.

Omar's Intellectual Antecedents.

ALL who wish to read Omar with intelligence will do
well to bestow a little attention on the main intellectual
currents of his time, the ideas and sentiments which
were fermenting in the minds of his contemporaries.
Some of these ideas acted on him by attraction, others
by repulsion; but in whichever way they acted, they
constituted the main factors, so to speak, of his opinions.
They may be grouped under the following four heads:
(1) the *Shari''at*, or sacred law; (2) *Hikmat*, philosophy,
(3) *Ma'rifat*, or mysticism; and (4) Poetry.

(1) *Shari'at*. The Persians never took kindly to
Arabian orthodoxy. In the 1st century A H their
dissent showed itself at the death of the Khalif 'Alí, in
the establishment of the great Shi'ite schism. Again,
in the 2nd century A H., when the descendants of Abbás,
mainly by Persian support, had ousted the Omayyads
and established the Khalifate in their own line, signs
of a fresh dissidence began to show themselves. For
a moment it seemed possible that the dogmatism of
Arabian theology might be tempered by an infusion of

Persian rationalism. The Arabian divines had started a doctrine somewhat similar to the bibliolatry of extreme Protestants in Europe, viz. the doctrine that the Koran was uncreated, and the Khalif Mamún was moved (no doubt by Persian influence) to issue his bull against it. But theology, always prone to obscurantism, soon gravitated back into the old ruts, and dogmatized in its accustomed strain on the unknowable mysteries which formed the "roots" of theological discussion

The first of these was predestination The Prophet, according to tradition, had warned his followers against speculating on this dangerous subject, but the theologians were not to be denied The Koran (as Canon Mozley remarked of the Bible*) is in one department of its language necessitarian, while in another it uses the language of free-will. Common sense would infer from this that its language is only popular, but this view could not be taken by theologians, who start with the axiom that every statement in the Koran is as exact as a proposition in Euclid. They were driven to accept one or other of the contradictory alternatives, and the bulk of them chose the former and maintained the doctrine of absolute predestination, or as they called it *jabr*, compulsion. Allah, they said, is the only Real Agent, *Fá'il i haqíqi*, and the seeming action of man is entirely determined by His will. It is true that the Mu'tazalites, the Broad Church theologians, held a somewhat qualified doctrine called *Kadr*, allowing some small scope to free-will, but they were always in a

---

* Mozley, "Augustinian Doctrine of Predestination,' p. 36.

minority and of small account   Of course, the extreme
predestinarian view raised the further question how
far the goodness of Allah was consistent with this compulsion, and to this no very satisfactory reply could be
given.   After their manner, the theologians first raised
a gratuitous difficulty, and then sought to explain it
by declaring it to be a mystery divinely ordained as a
trial to faith.

The second "root" was the promises and threats, i e.
the Prophet's Paradise and Hell   His full-flavoured
descriptions of these were probably mere expansions
of Talmudic or Millenarian apocalypses * ; and these
symbols were well suited to the unlettered Arabs of the
time, who indeed could not have understood anything
higher.† It was only when Persian culture began to
prevail that some of the broader-minded theologians
raised questions on the subject.

The third "root" was faith and reason ; and the
upshot of this discussion was, what it has always been
from the time of Job down to the present day, viz.
that the faithful may reason as much as they like,
subject to the inflexible condition that their reasonings
must always land them in the orthodox conclusions.‡

Other discussions there were about the Divine essence
and attributes, anthropomorphism, &c., dim anticipa-
tions of the discussions of our own time as to the

---

* See Renan, "Christianisme," vi , p. 138, and iv , pp 346 and
471

† The same plea may be made for Dante's grotesque Inferno.

‡ See Dr. Temple's remonstrance, dated 25th Feb 1861,
Tait s Life, vol 1 , p 220 (3rd edition)

difference of "regulative and speculative truths," as
Mansel calls them,* of mere symbolical conceptions
having only a relative truth, and of real conceptions
exactly representative of the Absolute.

(2) *Hikmat*, or philosophy. Wonder has been expressed at the suddenness with which the unlettered
Moslems, men of one book and of one idea, assimilated
the stores of Greek learning. But the marvel dis-
appears when the circumstances are taken into consideration. It was only when Persian influence had
obtained ascendancy in the new court at Baghdad that
this change began. By the aid of Syrian and Jewish
translators, Aristotle's Physics, Logic, and Metaphysics,
with the *Isagoge* of Porphyry and the glosses of Alexandrian commentators, the *Almajiste* of Ptolemy, the
medical works of Hypocrates and Galen, and the geometry
of Euclid, &c., were laid open to the investigation of
Moslem enquirers. They spared no pains to master all
this new learning, and the results may be seen in the
great Encyclopædia, *Ikhwán us Safa*, which was
compiled in the 4th century A H. As may be seen from
Dieterici's abstract of this work, "Die Welt-Seele," all
their metaphysics were strongly coloured by Neo-
platonist doctrines † Plotinus, ‡ the "Sheikh of the

---

* Mansel, "Bampton Lectures," 5th edition, p 90 , and
Spencer. "First Principles, ch ii , clause 9.

† According to Dr Bronh (Journal R A. S for April, 1901),
"Aristotle's Theology" is a paraphrase of the Ennea ls of
Plotinus   See also Schmolders, "Documenta Philosophiæ
Arabum."

‡ See Haarbrucker, "Schahrastáni's Religionsparthelen und
Philosophen-Schulen, vol ii , p 429, note 192 ff

Greeks," was the authority who mainly shaped their philosophy They took as their first principle his doctrine of the "One," the *Noumenon*, wherefrom the world of phenomena proceeded by successive "rayings-out" or emanations, viz , the *Logos* or *'Aql i kull*, the *Pneuma* or *Nafs i kull (Anima Mundi)*,* etc. This cosmogony they completed by carrying on the process of emanation through the seven heavenly spheres, the four elements, the three kingdoms of nature to man, the microcosm and summary of the whole Kosmos † The "One" they regarded as the only real existence, "deeply interfused" (to use Wordsworth's expression) in all the matter and all the force of the universe and in the mind of man.

It is true, as we learn from Ghazzáli and from Rumi, that some men of science held materialist (*dahri*) views, But the weightier exponents of *hikmat*, like the *Ikhwán us Safa* and Avicena, give no countenance to this shallow sciolism. The apparently mechanical movement of the heavenly bodies, for example, did not blind them to the existence of the Prime Mover, who started the universe on its course and maintains it from day to day ‡

---

* The later history of this conception has been admirably set forth by Renan in his "Averroes"

† See quatrains 120, 340, 355, 497.

‡ Their doctrine of the evolution of the soul from inorganic matter through vegetive and animal life, based on Aristotle's *De Anima*, presents some analogies with Mr H Spencer's doctrine of the evolution of consciousness It must not be confounded with metempsychosis, see *Masnavi*, 2nd edition, p 216, note

c

Whewell* does not rate their science, astronomy, &c, as highly as Gibbon He says they added nothing to what the Greeks taught them. Be this as it may, they certainly had mastered their lesson.

Their creed was probably that sketched in the *Dabistan* as "the religion of the philosophers," a religion based on reason, or supposed reason, and not on authority and blind imitation, *taqlíd*, and therefore one necessarily antagonistic to the Sharı́'at.

(3) *Ma'rifat*, or mysticism Sufism † took its rise about the end of the 1st century A.H, long before Persian influences came into play It was simply the personal religion, so to speak, of the devouter souls, who looked to the spirit more than to the letter, and craved for closer communion with the Deity than they seemed to find by means of the ordinary ceremonial observances They called themselves "interior men," *i e* men who strove to lead the inner life, "holy and humble men of heart", above all, *'Árifín, i e* Gnostics or knowers They loved to dwell on all the real or supposed immediate action of the Deity on the human soul—grace, spiritual illumination, the inner light, and the like

They were at issue with the orthodox theologians, whom they stigmatized as "men of externals," or men of the letter as opposed to the spirit. Their conception

---

* Whewell, "History of the Inductive Sciences," 3rd edition, vol 1, p 172.

† See the Introduction to my translation of the *Masnaví* of Jalaluddin Rumi, 2nd edition.

of the Deity, or, as they called him, "the Truth," *Al Haqq*, was more abstract than the orthodox conception of Allah, though retaining many of Allah's attributes, as for instance his omniscience, his mercy and vengence, *jamál* and *jalál*, and generally his "compulsion." But they could not stomach the orthodox views of Paradise and Hell, both because they conflicted with their doctrine of disinterested love, and because the only future state they recognised was one of complete absorption in "the Truth." The statements of the Koran on these points they explained away by allegorical interpretation, and they made free use of allegory to veil their own unorthodox doctrines * They practised asceticism with as much self-devotion as the early Christian monks, enjoyed visions like St Catherine and St. Theresa, and preached disinterested love with as much conviction as Mme. Guyon and Fénelon. It can hardly be denied that there was much genuine piety among such of them as were Sufis in reality as well as in name, but no doubt they were overprone to hysterical raptures and transports; and their contempt for the letter and the outward ordinance sometimes led them into antinomianism as pronounced as that of the Anabaptists of Munster.

Their position with regard to the philosophers was one of partial agreement and partial disagreement A comparison of Dieterici's "Die Welt-Seele" with

---

* An authentic explanation of this language, which pervades Persian poetry, is given in *Gulshan i Raz*, Answers 13 to 15.

Palmer's "Oriental Mysticism" * shows that in their ontology this agreement was almost complete The "Truth" was simply the "One" of Plotinus and the *Ikhwán us Safa*, with some infusion of personality. They differed from the philosophers in holding the possibility of immediate intuition of the "Truth" or Deity. In a word, they accepted the whole of Plotinus' doctrine, including his view of ecstasy, spiritual illumination, and ultimate union with the Deity, *henôsis* In modern language it may be said that they were the Gnostics, and the philosophers the Agnostics of the period

(4) Poetry After the Abbasides had established themselves at Baghdad, some of their Persian lieutenants, *e.g.* the Taharides and the Samanides, founded small national dynasties in the east of the Empire, and Persian culture, after two centuries of neglect, once more met with court favour Dr Ethé has traced this renaissance of Persian poetry with great industry and skill, but unfortunately his papers on the subject are very hard to come by However, a clear and graceful abstract of them has been given by Darmesteter in his "Origines de la Poesie Persane." The first great patron of the poets was Amir Nasr of Bokhara, and his chief laureate was the celebrated Rudagi who devoted himself to writing panegyrics of the Amir himself, and love-poetry for the ladies of the harem Some of the latter are full of pretty conceits, and the ladies must

* A summary of the *Maqsad i Aqsá* of 'Aziz bin Muhammad Nasafi (Haji Khalfa, vi 90).

have found them perfectly sweet. Narcissus eyes, tulip cheeks, cypress forms, bulbuls and so on, had then the charm of novelty, and the tune had not become wearisome by repetition on the barrel-organs of mere poetasters.

Abú Sa'íd bin Abí-l-Khair,* in the 5th century A H introduced a new strain. He was the first considerable writer of quatrains, and he used them to inculcate the mystical doctrines of the Sufis. He is also noteworthy as apparently the earliest poet who adopted their peculiar allegorical language. A contemporary of his, the celebrated Avicena,† employed the quatrain to express his philosophic criticism of life. Another poet, Hakím Kisáí,† of rather earlier date, had written a few quatrains on the same subject. About the same time, under the patronage of Mahmud of Ghazna, Firdausi gave voice to the reviving sense of Persian nationality in his great heroic poem, the *Shahnáma*. Darmesteter's account of this poetic renaissance is full enough for ordinary purposes, but his article, which originally appeared in the "Journal des Débats," betrays some of the defects incidental to such compositions, namely, too great straining after effect, and consequent sacrifice of balanced judgment to antithesis and point Thus, for instance, Omar is dealt with immediately after the saintly mystic Abú Sa'íd, and of course has to serve

---

* Dr Ethé has collected ninety-two of his quatrains from various *Tazkiras*. I have given translations of a few samples of these with others from the Bengal Asiatic Society's MS. in the Calcutta Review April 1896.

† Dr. Ethé has published some of these quatrains.

as a foil On the evidence of a single flippant and
offensive utterance (B. no 141) he is summarily gibbeted
without allowance for extenuating circumstances, and
the critic passes gaily on to the next item in the
calendar.

§ 5

Character of Omar's Poetry

OMAR was the product of his time, and each one of its
intellectual currents, all too briefly sketched in the last
section, met and mingled in his mind. The religion,
the philosophy, the mysticism and the poetry all had
their influence on him in varying proportions. Of
course, critics, ancient and modern alike, who judge him
by the criterion of popular shibboleths, pronounce him
to be an atheist and a materialist. But those who
bring candid intelligence to bear on his quatrains will
demur to this judgment. Whether under the Imam
Muwaffiq or some other divine, he was thoroughly
grounded in the *Shari'at* in his youth, and he carried
away from this teaching the firm conviction of the
Tauhíd, that is, the existence of the One God, the
Omnipresent power, *Fá'il i haqíqi*. This conviction
comes out again and again in his quatrains, and his
latest reported utterance shows that he held it to the
end of his life His studies in philosophy did not
destroy this conviction, but rather deepened it, though
they, of course, shook his faith in the dogmas of the
divines as to the nature and attributes of the One
Absolute Being. Like Mr. Herbert Spencer, he was at

one with the theologians in his conviction *that* the Absolute existed, but differed from them in holding that man could not know exactly *what* it was. In some quatrains he uses the current theological language, and speaks of the Absolute as the personal Allah; in others he uses the Sufi term, "the Truth," which is somewhat more abstract but, whatever his language, he never wavers in his assertion of the existence of the Absolute.

As regards the charge of materialism, Omar had read his science, mainly astronomy, in the light of his philosophy, and therefore was in no danger of falling into that crude realism which leads sciolists into materialism. He had thoroughly grasped the Greek doctrine that our senses give us information of phenomena only and that this knowledge is consequently no reliable criterion of "*Ding an sich*," or absolute existences (*Noumena*).* In his quatrains we constantly come across recognitions of the limitations of science, of its inability to fathom the beginning or end of the Kosmos, or to travel one step beyond the limits of human thought and comprehend the mysterious essence of the "Truth" Certainly Omar did not labour under the delusion that science had explained everything, and that the Absolute Omnipresent Power had been, so to speak, crowded out of the Kosmos Just so Huxley, in his well-known lecture on the "Physical Basis of Life," after stating the scientific view in terms of crude realism, was careful to warn his hearers that the

---

* See Ghazzáli's reflections on this point in Schmoldeis, "Écoles Philosophiques chez les Arabes," p 20

Absolute Being underlying all these physical phenomena is unknowable in any strict sense of knowing, and that the real origin and basis of life remain as much a mystery as they were before biologists began to speculate about them. It is as absurd to charge Omar with materialism as to impute the same blunder to Huxley or Herbert Spencer.

When we come to look into the subjects of Omar's quatrains, we find that a very large proportion of them may be classed as *shikáyat i Rózgár*, complaints of the wheel of heaven, or "the wheel of things," as it is called in the "Religio Medici." This topic was not a new one in Persian poetry, indeed it had been one of the commonplaces of poetry as far back as the times of Job and of Koheleth, "the weary King Ecclesiast." Ruskin classes artists as (1) Naturalists, those who try to give an objective representation of nature and human life, ignoring neither the good nor the evil, a representation undistorted, as far as may be, by the refraction of their own mental atmosphere; (2) the Purists, those who shut their eyes to all but the good and beautiful; and (3) those whom we may call Pessimists, who dwell by preference on the darker side. Omar undoubtedly belonged to the last class. He is never tired of dwelling on the chances and changes of this mortal life, on the ills flesh is heir to, life's brief duration, the swift passing of youth, the loss of friends, the limits of man's faculties, and on the vanity of life generally. Even the spirit-stirring memories of past national greatness, the Khosraus, Jamshéds and Farídúns, recently immortalized by Firdausi, only affect him as so many instances of the transitoriness of human greatness and the vanity of human glory. Human life seems to him but a "tale of sound and fury, told by an idiot and signifying nothing." "Out, out, brief candle," is to him the moral of the whole. And Omar would certainly have endorsed J S Mill's indictment of Nature, and Tennyson's description of her as "red in tooth and claw with ravin."

To these perplexing problems another class was added, namely, those suggested by his religious beliefs. Holding, as he did, the conviction that whatever occurred to man was the direct handiwork of the One Real Agent, the difficulty of accounting for the design of this divine action pressed upon him with overwhelming weight. As a convinced Unitarian he could not take refuge in the dualistic doctrine of his forefathers, who ascribed all the good to Ormuzd and all the evil to Ahrimán. Neither could he evade the difficulty by any such half-avowed Manicheeism as occasionally shows itself in the popular theology of the West No Ahrimán or Iblis * could be utilized by him to account for all the evils in the world, the plague, pestilence and famine, the storms and the earthquakes, the Borgias and the Catilines. The One Real Agent had to answer for all

These problems weighed upon him like a constant nightmare, and according to his varying moods he dealt

---

* In the *Masnavi* (p 95) there is an amusing expostulation by Iblis against being treated as the author of evil, and, on the Unitarian principle, he makes out a very good case for himself.

with them in three different spirits, which may be
distinguished as (1) the spirit of revolt, (2) the spirit
of the maxim "Eat and drink, for to-morrow we die",
and (3) the spirit of pious resignation

(1) The spirit of revolt. The solutions of the problems of life supplied by the Koran were for Omar in
the main impossible, and provoked him to dissent. The
character of Allah, as there set forth, was not one that
he could altogether accept. Allah's alleged revelations
seemed to him often plainly unworthy of the Supreme
Being. A special revelation, for instance, designed to
facilitate additions to the Prophet's harem,* was hardly
such as to gain implicit credence from him. He found
a marked contradiction between the revealed law and
the law of nature, which, *ex hypothesi*, proceeded from
one and the same authority † The doctrine of extreme
predestination was always "thrusting him into despe-
ration" (to use the language of our Article 17). He
could not appreciate the reasons for the excessive importance assigned to mere outward forms and cere-
monies Above all, the Prophet's Paradise and Hell,
an eternity of satiety or an eternity of torment, failed
to reach his conceptions of a future state. These old-
world symbols might have had an average adaptation
to the needs of the unlettered Arabs for whom they
were intended, but they were decidedly a stumbling-
block to a man of Omar's culture, and they provoked
him to scoffing and revolt. Hence what are known as

---

* See Koran xxxiii 49
† See quatrains 265, 432, 434, etc.

his *hufiiya* or infidel quatrains, a title of course bestowed on them by the orthodox. Quite in the spirit of the righteous Job he questions the justice of Allah s dealings with man. "Thy hands made me, yet Thou dost destroy me."* The heavenly Artisan creates a masterpiece and then, without apparent reason, dashes it to pieces † When Job's comforters urged him to confess that the calamities which had fallen upon him were the just punishment for sins he had committed, that patriarch asked them in his wrath, "Will ye talk deceitfully for God?" ‡ Will ye accuse me falsely to save Yahveh's credit? As Koheleth says, "There is one event to all, to him that sacrificeth and him that sacrificeth not." § Clean hands and a pure heart are no safeguard against misfortunes By what almost looks like a terrible irony, it is as often as not the most blameless lives that are stricken with grievous sufferings, sufferings beyond the power of human wit to devise or inflict, and which human skill is powerless to alleviate. And Koheleth comes to the conclusion that Yahveh has made things crooked, || and that none can make them straight

By Omar's time this difficulty had become augmented

---

* Job x 8   † See quatrain 290

‡ Job xiii 7, Revised Version   Renan translates "Voulez-vous pour Dieu tenir des discours iniques ? Et pour lui plaire proférer le mensonge?" Renan's 'Job," p. 53. See the whole discussion, Job iii -xxxi, specially xxvii 2–6

§ Ecclesiastes ix. 2, and see the rest of the passage.

|| See Ecclesiastes vii 13.

by the advance of the religious conception of the world
to come. In the times of Job and of Koheleth that
conception was limited to a vague idea of *Sheol*, the
shadowy under-world of the departed,* but now it had
been developed into an eternity of physical pleasures
or physical pains. The drama of human life was no
longer played out in one brief scene, but the action (for
the most part tragic) was carried on through ages
without end. In one sense it may be said that this
new world had been called into existence to redress the
inequalities of the old, but from another point of view it
served only to aggravate and accentuate the injustices
of this present life. This was the view Omar took of
it, and it lent additional poignance to his arraignment
of Allah's justice. The effects of that injustice were no
longer confined to the brief span of life on earth, but
extended to all eternity. "True," he says, "men are
only miserable erring slaves, yet who created them but
Thou?" Is all the blame justly chargeable to them
and none to their Creator? and is it just to punish
these helpless creatures of a day with an eternity of
torment? On this theme he dilates in many quatrains †
He nowhere mentions Eden or the snake, nor does he
offer forgiveness to Allah, but Fitz-Gerald's often-quoted
lines are an accurate reflection of the spirit in which
Omar treats the question. He regards life as a very
doubtful blessing, and at times, like Job, he expresses
his hatred of it. If he had the choice he would never

---

* See Job x 21, 22.

† See quatrains 471, 126, 311, &c.

have accepted it, and yet now he is here, he is hardly willing to fly from the evils he knows to others whose extent he cannot gauge.* The problems and paradoxes of life so bewilder and overwhelm him that he often relieves his overwrought feelings by what Ruskin calls the "grotesque" treatment of the subject. In sheer despair he breaks out into bitter jesting and grim or flippant levity. He is always dwelling on the base uses to which imperial Cæsar is put when turned into clay. He likens men to a company of pots, speculating as to their own origin and destiny, pronouncing some of their number to be vessels of honour and others vessels of wrath, and drawing such conclusions as they may as to the motives and designs of the great Potter. But for all his levity and flippancy, it is quite a mistake to class him with mere *frondeurs* like Voltaire and Heine. They warred against religion in every form, while Omar's revolt was only against what he regarded as the excrescences and misconceptions of religion. At bottom he was essentially religious, while they were essentially anti-religious.

(2) The *carpe diem* spirit. A very large proportion of the quatrains passing under Omar's name, perhaps nearly one-third, are conceived in this spirit. Their number is so large indeed, and so many are mere variations of others, that it is almost certain that the bulk of them must be imitations by other hands But, making all possible deductions on this score, there is a large residuum which is probably his handiwork. All

---

* See quatrain 190

these praises of wine and exhortations to live for the day were part of the "common form," as lawyers call it, of the poetry of the time; and long before, Koheleth had summed up his practical philosophy of life in the maxim that "there is nothing better for a man than that he should eat and drink and make his soul enjoy good in his labour." *   Both in his case and in Omar's this *carpe diem* philosophy seems to have been, at any rate partially, an outlet for the feeling of hopelessness of attaining to any deeper solution of the problems of life. It is quite a mistake to take these "gather ye roses while ye may" effusions as proofs that Omar was nothing more than an "old Mahomedan blackguard," as Carlyle called him.†   No doubt, like his predecessor Avicena, he was no ascetic, and he was by no means averse from getting out of life whatever it could give, but his constant exhortations to drink wine must not be taken too literally. A man who passed a life of study, and had mastered all the theology, the philosophy and the science of the time, could hardly have been the mere sot which a hasty reading of his bacchanalian effusions might lead one to suppose. Like Luther, he held that the man who abjures song, wine and ladies' society lives a fool his whole life long. In the matter of the last-named item, his practice was certainly much laxer than the great German reformer

---

* Ecclesiastes ii 24.

† The Sufis interpret all these quatrains allegorically, just as Christians do the "Song of Songs." Common sense negatives this explanation

would have approved but other times, other manners.
Like Koheleth, he is constantly insisting on the ex-
pedience of moderation in all things, "Be not righteous
overmuch, neither overmuch wicked, why shouldest
thou destroy thyself?"* and he agrees with that
authority in his views as to the vanity of inordinate
pursuit of power, pleasure or riches

In reading this class of his quatrains one is always
being reminded of Horace But there is a wide difference between the two men, Horace was an Epicurean
pure and simple. His master, Lucretius had thoroughly
disabused him of any faith in the intervention of the
gods in the affairs of men.† The black ox of Calvinism
had never trodden on his foot, and he sang his *carpe
diem* odes in pure lightness of heart But Omar, to
whom the idea of the Unseen was ever present, often
seems to have been prompted to sing his *carpe diem*
songs by his overwhelming sense of the inscrutableness
of the Divine action. They were, in fact, the reaction
from the melancholy growing out of baffled enquiries
after truth.

By the way, it is amusing to note how ready both
Horace and Omar are to cry "*Video meliora proboque*,"
&c, the moment they experience the "*amari aliquid*"
flowing from some too delicious draught, how the smart

---

* Ecclesiastes vii. 15–17. Renan translates "Tel juste périt
nonobstant sa justice ; et tel scélérat coule de longs jours nonobstant sa scélératesse. Ne sois pas trop juste, ... ne sois pas
non plus trop méchant" Renan, "L'Ecclésiaste," p 124

† See the fine description of the Epicurean gods in Tennyson's
"Lotus-eaters '

of the *après* invariably suggests to both a train of elevated moral reflections; and how Omar's cup-bearer, like Horace's Davus, is occasionally moved to take upon himself the office of Mentor.

Another point of similarity between the two poets is their common feeling for the charms of the country Some of Omar's so-called *Báháríya* quatrains are amongst the most attractive that he wrote. The first burst of Spring when, after having been "long in populous city pent," he sallied forth to enjoy its charms, was a theme he loved to dwell on The strip of verdure fringing the banks of some purling stream the bright blossoms of flowers and the jubilant songs of birds touched a responsive chord in his nature.

(3) The spirit of pious resignation. Some of the quatrains of this class occurring in the MSS. are almost certainly mere glosses originally written by pious readers on the margins as a protest against Omar's unorthodox views, and afterwards foisted into the text by uncritical copyists. But allowing for this, the number of devotional and mystical quatrains probably written by Omar amounts to ten or twelve per cent of the whole. Unless we are prepared to throw over the authority of all the MSS., including the most ancient ones, we must reckon with these devotional quatrains. Nor is it very difficult to account for them. His quatrains were not all written at one time, but at different periods ranging over a long life-time and were prompted by the varying moods of thought and feeling which swayed him from time to time Very possibly the *carpe diem* quatrains were the product of

his earlier years, and the devotional ones the expressions of his maturer sentiments   Thus Job, after
the rebellious utterances provoked by the first shock
of his calamities, settles down into pious agnosticism
and resignation to the will of Yahveh   He does
not pretend to fathom Yahveh's design, but he bows
to the inevitable. "Though He slay me, yet will I
trust in Him "*   And Koheleth, though he cannot
rise to the height of this exalted Quietism, still between
whiles preaches "the fear of the Lord." "We all
feel good when the organ blows," and Omar was like
the rest of us, full of lofty aspirations one minute
and relapsing into mundane frailties the next.† He
is very human, and honest enough not to try to hide
the fact. But for all his frailty, he had his moments
of aspiration. At such times his religious emotions
sometimes found vent in the orthodox phraseology
in which he had been trained in his youth   And
towards the latter part of his life he made a practice
of conforming to the requirements of the *Shar̄at*,
the daily prayers and ablutions and the pilgrimage.
Of course his enemies set this down to mere hypocrisy,
the homage rendered by an unrighteous man to
righteousness   But it may be that, Omar found
himself able to use these old symbols with more
sincerity than he got credit for   Of course he used
them with certain mental reservations. He could

---

* Job xiii 15

† This antinomy in human nature is well brought out in
Tennyson's "Two Voices," and Clough's "Dipsychus."

not attribute to them the saving efficacy which they
were commonly supposed to possess But symbols
he must use, and at times these symbols satisfied
his requirements. More frequently he expressed his
religious emotions in the language of the Sufis There
is no doubt that the writings of the saintly mystic
Abú Sa'íd had deeply impressed him And, as before
pointed out, the Ontology of the Sufis—their doctrine
as to the One Absolute Being, the One Real Agent,
and of the relation of this Being to the human soul—
was practically identical with his own philosophic
views. Sometimes he uses language which would
imply entire concurrence with the rest of the Sufi
doctrine, namely, the spiritual intuition, the ecstasy
and communion of the soul with the "One" But
these emotional utterances of his must not be pressed
too far. We must not run away with the idea that
he was himself a Sufi. Both by temperament and
conviction he was opposed to their asceticism, and
his eminently sceptical intellect could hardly accept
all their visions and inner voices as authentic messages
from the Deity. He must sometimes have asked
himself whether these visions might not be the mere
Brocken-spectres of the enthusiast's own personality
Even Wesley had his doubts whether "Satan did
not sometimes mock the work of grace."

Three other classes of Omar's quatrains must be
briefly noticed. The love-poems, singing the pangs
of separation and the joys of re-union with the loved
one, were part of the "common form" of the poetry
of the time, to which Abú Sa'íd had recently given

a deeper meaning by treating their language allegorically to denote the relation between the human soul
and the Deity. But these poems are of rare occurrence in Omar, who was certainly not a man much
given to sentiment of any kind.

The satires, *hajw,* on the other hand, are not
infrequent. " Rien ne soulage comme la rhetorique."
No doubt the dour old Záhids provoked him sorely,
but in his retaliation he was probably as unjust to
them as they were to him. The men of progress and
the men of prescriptive ideas can never be quite fair
to one another. If the dispute of reason and authority
had been formulated in one of those " contentions "
*munázira,** so much in fashion at the time, the weight
of argument would not perhaps have been found to
lie exclusively on either side. The Záhids might have
pressed the argument that the prescriptive ideas and
connected restraints ought not to be swept away until
some better and generally acceptable system had been
devised to take their place. Such a course could only
lead to moral and religious anarchy, and they might
have pointed the moral by reference to the recent
case of the brilliant Daqíqí, whom free-thinking and
other loose courses had brought to destruction.

One small class of his quatrains remains, namely,
what may be called the Gnomic quatrains,—pithy
moral dicta. He insists on the paramount duty of
charity and kindness to others, and this recalls the
better side of Voltaire's character, viz. his kindness

---

* Dr. Ethé has collected many of these in the *Tazkiras.*

to Calas and other victims of ecclesiastical perse-
cution. Also he has many sage reflections on the
importance of contentment and moderation in all
things

From this general summary of the quatrains it
is clear that Omar was not all *frondeur* and rebel,
nor all Epicurean, but was sometimes under the sway
of religious emotions; a man of varying moods, often
contradictory. We must not try to read into his
quatrains a consistent system of thought and sentiment.* This can only be done by shutting our eyes
to the reverse side of the shield. He was very human,
very frail, and a backslider, even when tried by his
his own, not too exalted, standards. The real interest
of the man for us lies in the fact that he gives us
so vivid a picture of the thoughts and the sentiments
fermenting in the minds of intelligent Persians eight
centuries ago When we translate his ideas, as far
as we can, into modern language, we are surprised
to find how closely analogous some of them are to
ideas and sentiments of our own time, and which
in our ignorance we are inclined to consider purely
modern discoveries. He has the touch of common
humanity which makes the ages kin. He has something of the large, direct utterance of our own
great Elizabethans He wrote in the early classic
period of Persian literature before euphuisms, "pen-

* Such an attempt was made in the "Kasidah of Haji
Abdu El-Yezdi," commonly ascribed to Sir R Burton (Quaritch,
1880).

flourishings," *kalambázı*, and artificial refinements had ousted simple and direct modes of expression *

In my first edition (1883) I acknowledged my indebtedness to Mr. Blochmann, M Nicolas, Professor Cowell, Dr. Ethé, M. Fagnan, Mr FitzGerald and Herr Bodenstedt. To these names I must now add those of Mr. H. Beveridge, Mr. C. E. Wilson, from whose review of my book in the *Academy* I gained many hints, and Mr Heron Allen, who has kindly allowed me to make use of his Bibliography.

---

* Daulat-Shah, writing in 892 A H, is a good illustration of the decadence of Persian taste at that time He says of Rudagi's beautiful Idyll on Bokhaia, that there was no court in his day which would not have rejected such simple verses with disgust (see Forbes Giammar, p 162).

ABBREVIATIONS.

A   Asiatic Society's MS , No. 1548.

B   Bodleian Library MS. of 865 A H

Bl   Blochmann's edition

C   Calcutta edition of 1252 A H

I   India Office MS , No 2420.

J   India Office MS , No 2486.

L.   Lucknow edition of 1878.

N   The edition of M Nicolas.

Bl , Prosody.   The Prosody of the Persians, by Blochmann, Calcutta. 1872.

Gladwin   The Rhetoric of the Persians, by Gladwin, Calcutta, 1801.

Lumsden.   A Grammar of the Persian language, by Lumsden, Calcutta, 1810.

Vullers   Grammatica linguæ Persicæ, scripsit I. A. Vullers, Gissæ, 1870.

Gulshan i Raz.   Text and translation of the Gulshan i Raz, by E H. Whinfield, London, 1880.

Masnavi.   Masnavi i Ma'navi of Jaláluddin Rumi, translated by E H Whinfield, 2nd edition, 1898

Ibn Khallikan.   Biographical Dictionary by Ibn Khallikan, translated by De Slane, Paris, 1843.

M   A MS. in my possession, written 1012 A H , containing selections from thirteen poets of the 5th to the 8th cent A H (868 pp)

S   The Bengal Asiatic Society's MS . No. 1398, of the Ruba'iyat of Abu Sa'id bin Abi 'l-Khair, containing 250 Ruba'is.

T   Munáját, or Invocations of Pir Ansari, with a few quatrains by him , some quatrains of Abu Sa'id with devotional glosses , and some quatrains of Omar Khayyam, &c Lithographed at Teheran

Ethé   Nachrichten von der Gesellschaft der Wissenschaften und der Universität zu Gottingen, 1873 (p 663), 1875 (p 555), 1882 (p. 122), Sitzungsberichte der Bayrischen Academie, 1875 (p. 145), 1878 (p 38), 1874 (p 133) &c

H   Haft Iqlim, written by Amin Ahmad Razi in 1002 A H

AK   Atash Kadah by Lutf 'Ali bin Aqa Khan, begun in 1174 A H.

Q   Tazkira, by Riza Quli Khan. 1284 A H

QUATRAINS

OF

OMAR KHAYYAM

QUATRAINS OF OMAR KHAYYAM

1.

At dawn a cry throughout the tavern shrilled,
"Arise my brethren of the revellers' guild,
   That I may fill our measures full of wine,
Or e'er the measure of our days be filled."

2.

Who was it brought thee here at nightfall, who?
Forth from the harem, in this manner, who?
   To him who in thy absence burns as fire,
And trembles like hot air, who was it, who?

Rubá'iyát, the *tashdíd* on the final *ye* of *rubá'í* is omitted
in Persian. Bl, Introduction to *Risála i Tarána* of Ághá
Ahmad 'Alí, p 1

1 Bl. C. L N A. I J. Bl. considers this quatrain
mystical.

رُباعِیاتِ حکِیم خَیّام

۱

آمد سَحَری ندا زِمیخانهٔ ما

کای رِندِ خراباتیِ دیوانهٔ ما

برخیز که پُر کُنیم پیمانه ز می

زان پیش که پُر کُنند پیمانهٔ ما

۲

امشب بَرِ ما مست که آورد ترا

وز پرده بدین دست که آورد ترا

نزدیکِ کسی که بیتو در آتش بود

چُون باد همی جست که آورد ترا

---

2. Bl. C. L. N. A. I. J. Bl. says the omission of the
copulative *wa* in line 4 is characteristic of Khayyam. In
line 4 I follow Blochmann's rendering. It may mean,
"when the wind blows."

3.

This world, our sometime lodging here below,
Doth yield us naught but store of grief and woe,
    And then, alas, with all our doubts unsolved,
And heavy-hearted with regret we go.

4.

Khaja! grant one request, and only one,
Wish me God-speed, and get your preaching
      done ;
    I walk aright, 'tis you who see awry ;
Go ! heal your purblind eyes, leave me alone.

5.

Arise ! and come, and of thy courtesy
Resolve my weary heart's perplexity,
    And fill my goblet, so that I may drink,
Or e'er they make their goblets out of me.

---

3. N.
4 Bl C L. N. A. I. J
5. Bl. C. L. N. A I. J. The heart is supposed to be

۳

این دهر که بُود بُدَّتی منزلِ ما
نامد بجز از بلا وغم حاصلِ ما
افسُوس که حل نگشت یک مشکلِ ما
رفتیم و هزار حسرت اندر دلِ ما

۴

ای خواجه یکی کام روا کُن مارا
دم در کش و در کارِ خُدا کُن مارا
ما راست رویم ولیک تو کج بینی
رو چارهٔ دیده کُن رها کُن مارا

۵

برخیز و بیا بیا برایِ دلِ ما
حل کن بجمالِ خویشتن مُشکلِ ما
یک کوزهٔ می بیار تا نوش کُنیم
زان پیش که کوزها کُنند از گلِ ما

6.

When I am dead, with wine my body lave,
For obit chant a bacchanalian stave,
   And, if you need me at the day of doom,
Beneath the tavern threshold seek my grave.

7.

Since no one can assure thee of the morrow,
Rejoice thy heart to-day, and banish sorrow
   With moonbright wine, fair moon! the moon
      in heaven
Will look for us in vain on many a morrow.

8.

Let lovers all distraught and frenzied be,
And flown with wine, and reprobates, like me;
   When sober, I find everything amiss,
But in my cups I say, "Let be, let be."

---

6.   Bl. C. L N. A I. J.   *Taut shudan* is Turani Persian.   Bl.

٦

چون فوت شوم بباده شوئید مرا

تلقین ز شراب و جام گوئید مرا

خواهید بروزِ حشر یابید مرا

از خاكِ درِ میکده جوئید مرا

٧

چُون عُهده نمیشود کسی فردارا

حالی خوش کن این دلِ پر سودارا

می نوش بنورِ ماه ای ماه که ماه

بسیار بتابد ونیابد مارا

٨

عاشق همه ساله مست و شیدا بادا

دیوانه وشوریده و رُسوا بادا

در هُشیاری غُصّهٔ هر چیز خوریم

ور مست شویم هرچه بادا بادا

---

7. Bl C. L. N. A B I J. Line 2 is in metre 14.

8. Bl. L. N. Line 3 is in metre 13.

9.

Why, in the name of Allah, set the wise
Their hearts upon this house of vanities ?
   Whene'er they think to rest them from their
      toils,
Death takes them by the hand, and says,
      "Arise."

10.

Men say the Koran holds all heavenly lore,
But on its pages seldom care to pore ;
   The lucid lines engraven on the bowl,—
That is the text they dwell on evermore.

11.

Blame not the drunkards, you who wine eschew,
Had I but grace, I would abstain like you,   .
   And mark me, vaunting zealot, you commit
A hundredfold worse sins than drunkards do.

---

9 Bl C. L N A. I
10. Bl L. N. A. B I J. Lines were engraven on the
bowl to measure out the draughts. Bl

٩

عاقل بچه اُمّید دریں شُوم سرا

بر دولتِ او نهد دل از بهرِ خدا

هرگاه که خواهد بنشیند از پا

گیرد اجاش دست که بالا بنما

١٠

قرآن که بهین کلام خوانند اورا

گه گاه نه بر دوام خوانند اورا

در خطّ پیاله آیتی روشن هست

کاندر همه جا مدام خوانند اورا

١١

گر می خوری طعنه مزن مستانرا

گر توبه دهد توبه کنم یزدانرا

تو فخر بدین کنی که من می خورم

صد کار کنی که می غُلامست آنرا

---

11. B1 C. L N A I. *Yazdáná*, an oath. *Ghulám*,
mere " children " compared to your sins. Comp B 3.

12.

What though 'tis fair to view, this form of man,
I know not why the heavenly Artisan
   Hath set these tulip cheeks and cypress forms
To deck the mournful halls of earth's divan.

13.

My fire doth yield no smoke-cloud here below,
My stock-in-trade no profit here below,
   And you, who call me tavern-hunter, know
There is indeed no tavern here below.

14.

Thus spake the idol to his devotee,
" How camest thou my worshipper to be ?
   " 'Twas for that he who gazeth through thine
      eyes
" Once with his beauty did illumine me."

---

12. Bl. C L. N. A I. *Tarab* here "grief"
13. Bl. C. L. N A I. J. The anacoluthon in line 3, and the missing rhyme before the *radíf*, or burden, in

١٢

هر چند که رنگ و بوی زیباست مرا

چون لاله رخ و چو سرو بالاست مرا

معلوم نشد که در طربخانهٔ خاک

نقّاش من از بهرِ چه آراست مرا

١٣

از آتشِ ما دود کجا بود اینجا

وز مایهٔ ما سود کجا بود اینجا

آنکس که مرا نامِ خراباتی کرد

در اصّل خرابات کجا بود اینجا

١۴

بت گفت به بت پرست کای عابدِ ما

دانی ز چه روی گشتهٔ ساجدِ ما

بر ما بجمال خود تجلّی کردست

آنکس که ز تُست ناظر ای شاهدِ ما

---

line 4 are characteristic of Khayyam. Bl.

14. L. Meaning, all is of God, even idols. See *Gulshan i Raz*, line 800.

15.

Whate'er thou doest, never grieve thy brother,
Nor kindle fumes of wrath his peace to smother;
    Dost thou desire to taste eternal bliss,
Vex thine own heart, but never vex another!

16.

O Thou! who moved by love and wrath as well,
When time began, didst fashion heaven and hell;
    Thou hast thy court in heaven, and I have
        naught,
Why not admit me in thy court to dwell?

17.

So many cups of wine will I consume,
Its bouquet shall exhale from out my tomb,
    And every one that passes by shall halt,
And reel and stagger with that mighty fume.

---

15   L. B. Line 1 is in metre 14.
16   Bl. L. The Sufis were fond of dwelling on the

١٥

تا بتّوانی رنجه مگردان کسرا

بر آتش خشم خویش منشان کسرا

گر راحت جاودان طمع میداری

میرنج همیشه و مرنجان کسرا

١٦

ای کرده بلطف و قهر تو صنع خدا

در عهد ازل بهشت و دوزخ پیدا

بزم تو بهشت است و مرا چیزی نیست

چونست که در بهشت ره نیست مرا

١٧

چندان بخورم شراب کین بوی شراب

آید ز تراب چون روم زیر تراب

تا بر سر خاک من رسد مخوری

از بوی شراب من شود مست و خراب

---

opposition between the beautiful (*jamál*) and terrible (*jalál*)
attributes of Deity. *Gulshan i Raz*, p. 27.

17. Bl. C. L. N. A. I. J.

18.

When seeking love pay court to every heart,
When once admitted seize the perfect heart;
    A hundred Ka'bas equal not one heart,
Seek not the Ka'ba, rather seek the heart!

19.

What time, my cup in hand, its draughts I drain,
And with rapt heart unconsciousness attain,
    Behold what wondrous miracles are wrought,
Songs flow as water from my burning brain.

20.

To-day is but one breathing space, quaff wine!
Thou wilt not see again this life of thine;
    So, as the world becomes the spoil of time,
Offer thyself to be the spoil of wine!

---

18 Bl C. L N A I. J. Line 2, "In the presence
seize the perfect heart." *Niyáz.* "lovers' entreaties" The
female saint Rabi'a expressed a similar sentiment.

١٨

در راهِ نیازِ هر دلی را دریاب

در کویِ حضورِ مُقبلی را دریاب

صد کعبهٔ آب و گل بیکدل نرسد

کعبه چه روی برو دلی را دریاب

١٩

روزی که بدست بر نهم جامِ شراب

وز غایتِ خرّمی شوم مست و خراب

صد مُعجزه پیدا کنم اندر هر باب

زین طبعِ چو آتیش سخنهای چو آب

٢٠

روزی که دو مهلتست می خورمِی ناب

کین عمرِ گذشته در نیابی دریاب

دانی که جهان رو بخرابی دارد

تو نیز شب و روز بمی باش خراب

---

19. **L. N.** *Sukhankáyŕ: Kasra i tausfíí* before the epithet *chu áb.* Lumsden, ii., p. 259. *Átísh*, archaic for *atash*.

20. **L. N.** *Do muhlat*, " inhaling and exhaling."

21.

We bend our necks beneath the yoke of wine,
Yea, risk our lives to gain the smiles of wine,
  While henchmen grasp the flagon by the
      throat,
And squeeze thereout the life-blood of the vine.

22.

Here in this tavern haunt I make my lair,
Pawning for wine, heart, soul, and all I wear,
  Without a hope of bliss, or fear of bale,
Rapt above water, earth and fire and air.

23.

Quoth fish to duck, " 'Twill be a sad affair,
If this brook leaves its channel dry and bare ; "
  To whom the duck, " When I am dead and
      roasted
The brook may mirage prove for aught I care."

---

21. L N   Line 3 is in metre 19.
22. Bl. C L N. A. B. I. J. Note the diphthong in *m ii*

٢١

ماائیم نهاده سر بفرمانِ شراب
جان کرده فدای لبِ خندانِ شراب
هم ساقیِ ما حلفِ صراحی در دست
هم بر لبِ ساغر آمده جانِ شراب

٢٢

ماائیم و می و مطرب و این کُنجِ خراب
جان و دل و جام و جامه در رهنِ شراب
فارغ ز امیدِ رحمت و بیمِ عذاب
آزاد ز باد و خاک وز آتش و آب

٢٣

با بط میگفت ماهئی در تب و تاب
باشد که بجوی رفته باز آید آب
بط گفت چو من و تو بگشتیم کباب
دود از پس مرگِ من چه دریا چه سراب

---

dissolved in scanning Bl, Prosody, 13

23. L. Meaning, *Après nous le déluge*

C

24.

From doubt to clear assurance is a breath,
A breath from infidelity to faith;
　　O precious breath! enjoy it while you may,
'Tis all that life can give, and then comes death.

25.

Ah! wheel of heaven to tyranny inclined,
'Twas e'er your wont to show yourself unkind:
　　And, cruel earth, if they should cleave your
　　　　breast,
What store of buried jewels they would find!

26.

My life lasts but a day or two, and fast
Sweeps by, like torrent stream or desert blast.
　　Howbeit of two days I take no heed,—
The day that's future and the day that's past.

---

24. Bl C. L N A I. J.
25. Bl C L N A I J. "Wheel of heaven," i e destiny fortune Sir Thomas Browne talks of the "wheel of

٢۴

از منزلِ کفر تا بدین یکنفس ست

وز عالمِ شک تا بیقین یکنفس ست

این یکنفسِ عزیز را خوش میدار

کز حاصلِ عمرِ ما همین یکنفس ست

٢٥

ای چرخِ فلک خرابی از کینهٴ تست

بیدادگری شیوهٴ دیرینهٴ تست

ای خاک اگر سینهٴ تو بشکافند

بس گوهرِ قیمتی که در سینهٴ تست

٢۶

این یک دو سه روزه نوبتِ عمر گذشت

چون آب بجوی بار و چون باد بدشت

هرگز غمِ دو روز مرا یاد نگشت

روزی که نیامدست و روزی که گذشت

---

things." In line 1 scan *khará biyaz.*

26. Bl. C. L. N. A. B. I. J. *Do sih roza* is an adjective. L.

27

That pearl is from a mine unknown to thee,
That ruby bears a stamp thou canst not see.

  The tale of love some other tongue must tell,
All our conjectures are but phantasy.

28.

Now that with young desires my breast is rife,
I quaff my wine, it adds a zest to life,

  Chide not at wine for all its bitter taste,
That bitterness sorts well with human life.

29.

O soul! whose lot it is to bleed with pain,
And daily change of fortune to sustain.

  Into this body wherefore didst thou come,
Seeing thou must so soon go forth again?

_ _ _ _ _ _ _ _   _   _ _   _   _ _   _   _

27. Bl L N. *Kíní, yá i balaí.* Bl, Pros. 7. Or,
perhaps, *yí i laukú.* See note to No 373 Meaning, real
love of God differs from the popular idea of it. Bl.

۲۷

آن لعلِ گران بها زكانی دگر ست
وان درّ یكانه را نشانی دگر ست
اندیشهٔ این وآن خیالِ من وتست
افسانهٔ عشق از زبانی دگر ست

۲۸

امروز كه نوبتِ جوانیّ من ست
می نوشم از آنكه كامرانیّ من ست
عیبش مكنید اگرچه تلخ ست خوش ست
تلخ ست از آنكه زندگانیّ من ست

۲۹

ای دل چو نصیبِ تو همه خون شدنست
احوالِ تو هر لحظه دگر گون شدنست
ای جان تو درین تنم چه كار آمدهٔ
چون عاقبتِ كارِ تو بیرون شدنست

28. Bl. C. L. N. A. B. I. J. Bl. notes, "Regarding the
tashdíd on *jawání*, see my Prosody, p. 11."
29. Bl. C. L. N. A. I. J.

30.

To-day is thine to spend, but not to-morrow,
Counting on morrows breedeth naught but
    sorrow ;
  Oh ! squander not this breath that heaven
    hath lent thee,
Nor make too sure another breath to borrow !

31.

'Tis labour lost thus to all doors to crawl,
Take thy good fortune, and thy bad withal :
  Know for a surety each must play his game,
As from the box of fate the dice may fall.

32.

This jug did once, like me, love's sorrows taste,
And bonds of beauty's tresses once embraced,
  This handle, which you see upon its side,
Has many a time twined round a slender waist !

---

30   Bl C. N A B I   In line 4, scan *Ki bákíyi 'umr írí.*
Bl , Prosody, 11.
  31.   Bl. C. L N. A. I. J.   *Naksh*, the dots on dice.

۳۰

امروز ترا دست رسی فردا نیست
واندیشهٔ فردات بجز سودا نیست
ضایع مکن ایندم ار دلت شیدا نیست
کین باقیِ عمررا بقا پیدا نیست

۳۱

از هرزه بهر دری نمیباید تاخت
با نیك و بدِ زمانه میباید ساخت
از طاسكِ چرخ و کعبتینِ تقدیر
هر نقش که پیدا شود آن باید باخت

۳۲

این کوزه چو من عاشقِ زاری بودست
در بندِ سرِ زلفِ نگاری بودست
این دسته که در گردنِ او می بینی
دستیست که بر گردنِ یاری بودست

33.

Days changed to nights, ere you were born,
  or I,
And on its business ever rolled the sky ;
  See you tread gently on this dust, perchance
'Twas once the apple of a beauty's eye.

34.

Pagodas, like as mosques, are homes of prayer,
'Tis prayer that church-bells chime unto the air.
  Yea, Church and Ka'ba, Rosary and Cross
Are all but divers tongues of world-wide prayer.

35.

'Twas writ at first, whatever was to be,
By pen unheeding bliss or misery,
  Yea, writ upon the tablet once for all,
To murmur or resist is vanity.

---

33 C L N A I J. *Nihâye, yá i tauhír*
34 Bl. C L N A I J. *Scan bandágiyast.* Bl Meaning, forms of faith are indifferent

٣٣

پیش از من و تو لیل و نهاری بودست
گردنده فلك زبهرِ کاری بودست
زینهار قدم بخاك آهسته نهی
کان مردمك چشمِ نـگاری بودست

٣٤

بتخانه و کعبه خانهٔ بندگیست
ناقوس زدن ترانهٔ بندگیست
زنّار وکلیسیا و تسبیح وصلیب
حقّا که همه نشانهٔ بندگیست

٣٥

بر لوح نشانِ بودنیها بوده است
پیوسته قلم ز نیك و بد آسوده است
اندر تقدیر هر چه بایست بداد
غمِ خوردن و کوشیدنِ ما بیهوده است

<hr/>

35. C. L. N. A. B. I. J. Meaning, the divine decree or destiny is inexorable. Scan *búd ast*, dropping silent *he*, and *alif i wasl*.

36.

There is a mystery I know full well,
Which to all, good and bad, I cannot tell:
   My words are dark, but I may not unfold
The secrets of the " station " where I dwell.

37.

No base or light-weight coins pass current here.
From these a broom has swept our dwelling
      clear ;
   Forth from the tavern comes a sage, and
      cries,
" Drink ! ere ye sleep through ages long and
      drear."

38.

With outward seeming we can cheat mankind,
But to God's will we can but be resigned :
   The deepest wiles my cunning e'er devised.
To shirk divine decrees no way could find.

---

36   Bl C L N A. I J. *Hâlé*, a state of ecstasy

37   Bl L N. Meaning, Mollas' fables will not go down
with us.

٣٦

با هر بد و نیك راز نـتّوانم گـفت،
كوته سخنم دراز نـتّوانم گـفت
حالی دارم كه شرح نـتّوانم داد
رازی دارم كه باز نـتّوانم گـفت

٣٧

با ما درم قلب نمیگیرد جفت
جاروب طربخانهء ما پاك برُفت
پیری ز خرابات برون آمد و گفت
می خور كه بعمرهات میباید خفت

٣٨

با حكم خدا بجز رضا در نـگـرفت
با خلق بجز روی و ریا در نـگـرفت
هر حیله كه در تصوّرِ عقل آید
كردیم ولیك با قضا در نـگـرفت

---

38. L. N. Meaning, weakness of human rule compared
to the strength of divine decrees.

39.

Is a friend faithless? spurn him as a foe,
But on trustworthy foes respect bestow;
   Hold healing poison for an antidote,
And baneful sweets for deadly evel know.

40.

No heart is there, but bleeds when torn from
     Thee,
No sight so clear but craves Thy face to see;
   And though perchance Thou carest not for
     them,
No soul is there, but pines with care for Thee.

41.

Sobriety doth rob me of delight,
And drunkenness doth drown my sense out-
     right;
   There is a middle state, it is my life,
Not altogether drunk, nor sober quite.

---

39 L N   These gnomic epigrams are not common
in Khayyam.

40   C L N. A I J   *Jigar*, the liver, was considered
to be the seat of love

٣٩

بیگانه اگر وفا کند خویشِ من است
ور خویش خطا کند بداندیشِ من است
گر زهر موافقت کند تریاکست
ور نوش مُخالفت کُند نیشِ من است

۴۰

پر خون ز فراقت جگری نیست که نیست
شیدایِ تو صاحبنظری نیست که نیست
با آنکه نداری سرِ سودایِ کسی
سودایِ تو در هیچ سری نیست که نیست

۴۱

تا هشیارم طرب ز من پنهان است
چون مست شدم در خردم نقصان است
حالیست میانِ مستی و هشیاری
من بندهٔ آن که زندگانی آنست

41. C. N. I. *Masti o:* scan *mastiyo*. The Epicurean golden mean. See Ecclesiastes vii. 16, 17: "Be not righteous overmuch: be not overmuch wicked,' &c.

42.

Behold these cups ! Can He who deigned to
    make them,
In wanton freak let ruin overtake them,
    So many shapely feet and hands and heads,—
What love drove Him to make, what wrath to
    break them ?

43.

Death's terrors spring from baseless phantasy,
Death yields the tree of immortality :
    Since 'Isa breathed new life into my soul,
Eternal death has washed its hands of me !

44.

Like tulips in the spring your cups lift up,
And, with a tulip-cheeked companion, sup
With joy your wine, or e'er this azure wheel
With some unlooked for blast upset your cup.

---

42 C. N. A. B 1 J *Piyálá, a cup* So Job, " Thy
hands have made me yet thou dost destroy me '

۴۲

ترکیبِ پیاله‌ء که درهم پیوست
بشکستنِ آن کجا روا دارد مست
چندین سر وپایِ نازنین وکف ودست
از مهرِ چه ساخت و بکینِ چه شکست

۴۳

ترسِ اجل و وهمِ فنا مستیِ تست
ورنه ز فنا شاخِ بقا خواهد رُست
تا از دمِ عیسوی شدم زنده بجان
مرگِ ابد از وجودِ من دست بشست

۴۴

چون لاله بنوروز قدح گیر بدست
با لاله رخی اگر ترا فرصت هست
می نوش بخرّمی که این چرخِ کبود
ناگاه ترا چو باد گرداند پست

---

43   L. N   Meaning, the Sufi doctrine of *Baká ba'd ul*
faná. See *Gulshan i Raz*, p. 31.

44   C L N A I J.

45.

Fate will not bend to humour man's caprice,

So vaunt not human powers, but hold your
peace:

    Here must we stay, weighed down with grief
for this,

That we were born so late, so soon decease.

46.

Khayyam! why weep you that your life is bad?

What boots it thus to mourn? Rather be glad.

    He that sins not can make no claim to mercy,

Mercy was made for sinners—be not sad.

47.

All mortal ken is bounded by the veil,

To see beyond man's vision is too frail;

    Yea! earth's dark bosom is his only home:—

Alas! 'twere long to tell the doleful tale

---

45 C L. N A. I. J. Meaning the futility of striving
against predestination. _Ink, for áukı. Bl. Prosody, 13
I omit silent _he_ in transliteration, as it only shows the preceding consonant has a vowel.

۴۵

چون کار نه بر مرادِ ما خواهد رفت
اندیشهٔ جهدِ ما کجا خواهد رفت
پیوسته نشسته ایم از حسرتِ آنك
دیر آمده ایم و زود میباید رفت

۴۶

خیّام زبهرِ گنه این ماتم چیست
وز خوردنِ غم فایده بیش وکم چیست
آنرا که گنه نکرد غفران نبود
غفران زبرایِ گنه آمد غم چیست

۴۷

در پردهٔ اسرار کسی را ره نیست
زین تعبیه جانِ هیچ کس اگه نیست
جز در دلِ خاكِ تیره منزلگه نیست
افسوس که این فسانها کوته نیست

---

46. C. L. N. A. B. I. See note on No. 130.
47. C. L. N. A. B. I. J.

48.

This faithless world, my home, I have surveyed,
Yea, and with all my wit deep question made,
    But found no moon with face so bright as
        thine,
No cypress in such stateliness arrayed.

49.

In synagogue and cloister, mosque and school,
Hell's terrors and heaven's lures men's bosoms
        rule,
    But they who master Allah's mysteries,
Sow not this empty chaff their hearts to fool.

50.

You see the world, but all you see is naught,
And all you say, and all you hear is naught,
    Naught the four quarters of the mighty
        earth,
The secrets treasured in your chamber naught

---

48. L. N
49 C L N A. B. I. J   Meaning, souls re-absorbed in

۴۸

در عالمِ بیوفا که منزلگهِ ماست
بسیار بجستم بقیاسی که مراست
چون رویِ تو ماه نیست روشن گفتم
چون قدِّ تو سرو نیست میگویم راست

۴۹

در صومعه و مدرسه و دیر و کنشت
ترسنده ز دوزخند و جویایِ بهشت
آنکس که ز اسرارِ خدا با خبر است
زین تخم در اندرونِ خود هیچ نکشت

۵۰

دنیا دیدهی و هر چه دیدی هیچ است
وان نیز که گفتی و شنیدی هیچست
سرتا سرِ آفاق دویدی هیچ است
وان نیز که در خانه خزیدی هیچ است

---

the Divine essence have no concern with the material heaven
and hell.

50. L. N. Meaning, all phenomena are illusion (*Maya*).

51.

A sage gave counsel, " Wherefore life consume

In sleep ? Can sleep make pleasure's roses
  bloom ?

Forgather not with death's twin-brother sleep.

Thou wilt have sleep enough within thy tomb!"

52.

If the heart knew life's secrets here below,

At death 't would know God's secrets too, I
  trow ;

But, if you know naught here, while still
  yourself,

To-morrow, stripped of self, what can you know ?

53

On that dread day, when wrath shall rend the
  sky,

And darkness dim the bright stars' galaxy,

I'll seize the Loved One by the skirt, and cry,

" Why hast Thou doomed these guiltless ones
  to die ?"

---

51   C L N A B I J   So Homer, Καιψη τοι θα-
νατοιο

52   C L. N. A. I   In line 2 scan Ìíihí   BI, Prosody,
p 7

۵۱

در خواب بُدم مرا خردمندی گفت

کز خواب کسی را گل شادی نشکفت

کاری چکنی که با اجل باشد جفت

می خور که بزیرِ خاك میباید خفت

۵۲

دل سرِّ حیات اگر کماهی دانست

در موت هم اسرار الهی دانست

اکنون که تو با خودی ندانستی هیچ

فردا که زخود روی چه خواهی دانست

۵۳

روزیکه شود اذا السماءُ انفطرَت

وانندم که شود اذا النجوم انکدرت

من دامنِ تو بگیرم اندر عرصات

گویم صنما بائّ ذنبٍ قتلَت

---

53. C L. N. A. I. J. See Koran, lxxxii. 1. Note th
alif i wasls in lines 1 and 2. In line 4 scan *kata lat*, tran
posing the last vowel. Bl., Prosody, p. ii.

54.

To knaves Thy secret we must not confide,
To comprehend it is to fools denied,
　　See then to what hard case Thou doomest
　　　　men,
Our hopes from one and all perforce we hide.

55.

Cupbearer! what though crooked fates betide
　　us,
And a safe resting-place be here denied us,
　　So long as the bright wine-cup stands before
　　　　us,
We have the very Truth itself to guide us.

56.

Long time in wine and rose I took delight,
But found my business never went aright ;
　　Since wine could not accomplish my desire,
I have abandoned and forsworn it quite.

---

54. C L N. A. B I. There is a variation of this,
beginning *Asrár i jahán.* It refers to the esoteric Sufi
doctrine *Bínísh*, poetical contraction for *Bínígar.*

۵۴

سرّ از همه ناکسان نهان باید داشت

راز از همه ابلهان نهان باید داشت

بنگر که بجای مردمان خود چه کنی

چشم از همه مردمان نهان باید داشت

۵۵

ساقی چو زمانه در شکست من و تست

دنیا نه سراچهٔ نشست من و تست

گر زانکه میان من و تو جام می است

میدان بیقین که حق بدست من و تست

۵۶

عمری بگل و باده برفتیم بگشت

یک کار من از دور جهان راست نگشت

از می چو نشد هیچ مرادی حاصل

از هرچه گذشتیم گذشتیم گذشت

<hr>

55. C. L. N. A. I. In line 3 scan *māyāst*. Bl., Prosody,
p. 13, and note *tashdíd* on *Hakk* dropped. Ibid, p. iv.
56. C. L. N. A. I. J.

57.

Bring wine ! my heart with dancing spirits
        teems,
Wake ! fortune's waking is as fleeting dreams :
    Quicksilver-like our days are swift of foot,
And youthful fires subside like torrent streams.

58.

Love's devotees, not Moslems here you see,
Not Solomons, but ants of low degree :
    Here are but faces wan and tattered rags,
No store of Coptic cloth, or silk have we.

59.

My law it is in pleasure's paths to stray,
My creed to shun the theologic fray :
    I wedded Luck, and offered her a dower,
She said, " I want none, so thy heart be gay "

---

57. C. L N A I. J. In line 3 scan *bedáráyi*
58. L. N   For the story of Solomon and the ants, see

۵۷

می در کفِ من نه که دلم در تابست
وین عمرِ گریز پای چون سیمابست
برخیز که بیداریِ دولت خوابست
دریاب که آتشِ جوانی آب است

۵۸

ما کافرِ عشقیم و مسلمان دگرست
ما مورِ ضعیفیم و سلیمان دگرست
از ما رخِ زرد و جامهٔ کهنه طلب
بازارچهٔ قصب فروشان دگرست

۵۹

می خوردن و شاد بودن آئینِ منست
فارغ بودن ز کفر و دینِ دینِ منست
گفتم بعروسِ دهر کابینِ تو چیست
گفتا دلِ خرّمِ تو کابینِ من است

Koran, xxvii. 18. *Kasab*, linen made in Egypt.
59. C. L. N. A. I. J.

60.

From mosque an outcast, and to church a foe.
Out of what clay did Allah form me so ?
　Like sceptic monk, or ugly courtesan,
No hopes have I above, no joys below.

61.

Men's lusts, like house-dogs, still the house
　　distress
With clamour, barking for mere wantonnes :
　Foxes are they, and sleep the sleep of hares :
Crafty as wolves, as tigers merciless.

62.

You turf, fringing the margent of the stream,
As down upon a cherub's lip might seem,
　Or growth from dust of buried tulip cheeks :
Tread not that turf with scorn, or light esteem !

---

60 C. L N A I. J. *Ummed* has the *tashdid ob metium*
Bl , Prosody, 9 Line 2 is in metre 17 *Gil i mará* for *gil
i man id*, Vullers, pp 173 and 193.

٦.

نی لایقِ مسجدم نه درخورْدِ کنشت

ایزد داند گِلِ مرا از چه سرشت

چون کافرِ درویشم و چون قحبهٴ زشت

نی دین و نه دنیا و نه امّیدِ بهشت

٦١

نفست بسگِ خانه همی ماند راست

جز بانگِ میان تهی از او هیچ نخواست

روبه صفتست و خوابِ خرگوش دهد

آشوبِ پلنگِ دارد و گرگِ دغاست

٦٢

هر سبزه که در کنارِ جوئی رستست

گوئی ز لبِ فرشته خوئی رستست

هان بر سرِ سبزه پا بخواری ننهی

کان سبزه بخاکِ لاله روئی رستست

---

61. C. L. N. A. I. J. "Sleep of hares," deceit.

62. C. L. N. A. I. J. *Juyiy:* the *yá* of *júy* is hamzated
because followed by another *yá.* Vullers, p. 24.

63.

Hearts with the light of love illumined well,
Whether in mosque or synagogue they dwell,
    Have *their* names written in the book of love,
Unvexed by hopes of heaven or fears of hell.

64.

One draught of wine outweighs the realm of
        Tús,
Throne of Kobád and crown of Kai Kaús;
    Sweeter are sighs that lovers heave at morn,
Than all the groanings zealot throats produce.

65.

Though Moslems for my sins condemn and
        chide me,
Like heathen to my idol I confide me;
    Yea, should I perish of a drunken bout,
I'll call on wine, whatever doom betide me.

---

63 C L N A. I. J.   Compare Hafiz, Ode 79:
" Wherever love is, there is the light of the Beloved's face '

٦٣

هر دل که در او نورِ محبّت بسرشت
گر ساکنِ مسجد است وگر ز اهلِ کنشت
در دفترِ عشق هر که را نام نوشت
آزاد ز دوزخ است و فارغ ز بهشت

٦٤

یکجرعهٔ می زملکِ کاووس بهست
وز تختِ قباد و ملکتِ طوس بهست
هر ناله که عاشقی بر آرد بسحر
از نعرهٔ زاهدانِ سالوس بهست

٦٥

هر چند که از گناه بدبختم و زشت
نومید نیم چو بت پرستان ز کنشت
امّا سحری که میرم از مخموری
می خواهم و معشوقه چه دوزخ چه بهشت

---

64. C. L. N. A. I. J. *Kawús* is the old spelling.
65. L. N. See a variation of this below, No. 111.

66.

In drinking thus it is not my design
To riot, or transgress the law divine,
    Nay, to attain deliverance from self
Is the sole cause I drink me drunk with wine.

67.

Drunkards are doomed to hell, so men declare,
Believe it not, 'tis but a foolish scare;
    Heaven will be empty as this hand of mine,
If none who love good drink find entrance
        there.

68.

'Tis wrong, according to the strict Korán,
To drink in Rajab, likewise in Sha'bán,
    God and the Prophet claim those months as
        theirs;
Was Ramazán then made for thirsty man?

---

66. C L N A I J. Perhaps a hit at the Suh's doctrine of alienation from self.

67 C L N. A l. J. Line 4 is in metre 17. "If sack

٦٦

می خوردنِ من نه از برایِ طربست

نز بهرِ فساد وترکِ دین و ادبست

خواهم که ز بیخودی بر آرم نفسی

می خوردن ومست بودنم زین سببست

٦٧

گویند که دوزخی بود مردمِ مست

قولیست خلاف دل در او نتوان بست

گر عاشق و مست دوزخی خواهد بود

فردا باشد بهشت همچون کفِ دست

٦٨

گویند مخور باده که شعبان نه رواست

نه نیز رجب که آنمه خاصّ خداست

شعبان و رجب ماهِ خدا هست و رسول

ما در رمضان خوریم کان خاصّهٔ ماست

---

and sugar be a sin, God help the wicked."

68. C. L. N. A. I. J. The point, of course, is that Ramazán is the Muhammadan Lent.

69.

Now Ramazán is come, no wine must flow,
Our simple pastimes we must now forego,
    The wine we have in store we must not
        drink,
Nor on our mistresses one kiss bestow.

70.

What is this world ?   A caravan-serai.
The haunt of alternating night and day,
    The leavings of a hundred Jamshed's feasts,
The couch whereon a hundred Bahrams lay !

71.

Now that your roses bloom with flowers of
    bliss,
To grasp your goblets be not so remiss ;
    Drink while you may ! Time is a treacherous
        foe,
You may not see another day like this.

---

69. L N
70. Bl. C L N. A I J   *Wámánda*, " leavings "

٦٩

آمد رمضان و موسمِ بادہ برفت
دورِ می ناب و راہِ ساده برفت
هر باده که داشتیم ناخورده بمانّد
هر قحبه کہ یافتیم ناگاہ برفت

٧٠

این کهنہ رباطرا کہ عالم نامست
آرامگہِ ابلقِ صبح و شام است
بزمیست کہ واماندهء صد جمشید است
گوریست کہ تکیہ گاہ صد بهرامست

٧١

اکنون کہ گلِ سعادتت بر بار است
دستِ تو ز جامِ می چرا بیکار است
می خور کہ زمانہ دشمنِ غدّار است
دریافتنِ روزِ چنین دشوار است

---

71 Bl C. L N. A. I. J *Bar bár*, "blooming, on the branch," *i e* you are still young Bl

E

72.

In these proud halls where Bahram once held
    sway
The wild roes drop their young and tigers stray,
   And that imperial hunter in his turn
To the great hunter Death is fallen a prey

73.

Down rain the tears from skies enwrapt in gloom,
Without this wine, the tulips could not bloom !
   As now these flowerets yield delight to me,
So shall my dust yield flowers,—God knows for
    whom.

74.

To-day is Friday, as the Moslem says,
Drink then from bowls served up in quick
    relays :
   Suppose on common days you drink one
    bowl,
To-day drink two, for 'tis the prince of days.

72　Bl C L N A I J.　Ibid.　see Bl , Pros. 11
73　Bl C L N A I J　In line 4 tá is the " ta i tap '-
hu, meaning ' I do not know whether,' ' perhaps '　Bl

٧٢

آن قصر که بهرام درو جام گرفت
آهو بره کرد و شیر آرام گرفت
بهرام که گور میگرفتی بکمند
دیدی که چگونه گور بهرام گرفت

٧٣

ابر آمد و باز بر سر سبزه گریست
بی باده ارغوان نمی باید زیست
این سبزه که امروز تماشاگه ماست
تا سبزهٔ خاک ما تماشاگه کیست

٧۴

امروز که آدینه مر اورا نام است
می نوش کن از قدح چه جای جامست
در روز اگر یکقدح می خوردی
امروز دو خور که سیّد الأیّامست

---

74. Bl. C. L. N. A. I. J.   Friday is the day " of assembly," or Sabbath.

75.

The *very* wine a myriad forms sustains,
And to take shapes of plants and creatures
    deigns;
    But deem not that its essence ever dies,
Its forms may perish, but its self remains.

76.

These people's fire gives only smoke; I swear,
For my well-being not a soul doth care;
    With hands, fate makes me lift up in despair,
I grasp men's skirts, but find no succour there.

77.

This bosom friend, on whom you so rely,
Seems to clear wisdom's eyes an enemy,
    Choose not as friends the people of to-day,
Their converse is a plague 'tis best to fly.

---

75   Bl C L N A I J   On this Bl notes "The Arabic
form *haymcán* is required by the metre"   And *swear* is the
Arabic plural, used as a singular   Bl , Prosody, 5   Wine
means the divine "*Noumenon*."   *Gulshan i Ráz*, 825

٧٥

آن باده که قابلِ صُوَرهاست بذات
گاهی حَیَوان همی شود گاه نبات
تا ظن نبری که هست گردد هیهات
موصوف بذاتست اگر نیست صفات

٧٦

از آتشِ این طائفه جز دودی نیست
وز هیچ کسم امیدِ بهبودی نیست
دستی که ز دستِ چرخ بر سر دارم
در دامنِ هرکه میزنم سودی نیست

٧٧

آنکس که بجملگی ترا تکیه بروست
گر چشمِ خرد باز کنی دشمنت اوست
آن به که درین زمانه کم گیری دوست
با اهلِ زمانه صحبت از دور نکوست

---

76. Bl. C. L. N. A. I. J. Scan *tayīfa*.
77. Bl. C. L. N. A. I. J. The MSS. transpose the lines
Literally, " Their society is good at a distance."

78.

O foolish one! this moulded earth is naught,
This particoloured vault of heaven is naught;
    Our sojourn in this seat of life and death
Is but one breath, and what is that but naught?

79.

Get minstrel, wine and Houri, if you can,
A green nook by a streamlet, if you can,
    And seek naught better; babble not of hell,
But find a better heaven, if you can.

80.

A sage I saw to tavern-house repair,
Bearing a wine-cup, and a mat for prayer;
    I said, "O Shaikh, what does this conduct
        mean?"
Said he, "Go drink! the world is naught but
        air."

---

78   Bl. L N.   *Shakl i mujassam.* 'the earth'   Bl.
79   Bl C. L N. A I. J.   *Dozakh i farsúda,* 'an old

٧٨

ای بیخبر این شکلِ مجسّم هیچ است
وین طارمِ نُه سپهرِ ارقم هیچ است
خوش باش که در نشیمنِ کون و فساد
وابستهٔ یکدمیم و آنهم هیچ است

٧٩

با مطرب و می حور سرشتی گر هست
با آبِ روان کنارِ کشتی گر هست
به زین مطلب دوزخِ فرسوده متاب
حقّا که جز این نیست بهشتی گر هست

٨٠

پیری ز خرابات برون آمد و مست
سجّاده بدوش و کاسهٔ باده بدست
گفتم شیخا ترا چه حال آمد پیش
گفتا می خور که کارِ عالم باد است

81.

The Bulbul to the garden winged his way,
Viewed lily cups, and roses smiling gay,
   Cried in ecstatic notes, " Enjoy your life,
You never will re-live this fleeting day."

82.

Thy body's like a tent which for a space
Thy spirit doth with royal presence grace :
   When he departs comes the tent-pitcher Death.
Strikes it, and moves to a new halting-place.

83.

Khayyam, who long time tents of science wrought.
Sank in the kiln of grief, and fire he caught :
   The shears of doom then cut his thread of life.
And Death the broker sold him off for naught.

---

81. N. The MSS have a variation of this, beginning
Bulbul chu. Jám . . . rá See Bl. Prosody p 12
82. C. L N A I J. *Manzil*, in line 2, 'lodging', in

٨١

چون بلبلِ مست راه در بستان یافت

رویِ گل و جامِ باده را خندان یافت

آمد بزبانِ حال در گوشم گفت

دریاب که عمرِ رفته را نتّوان یافت

٨٢

خیّام تنت بخیمهٴ ماند راست

سلطان روح است و مَنزِلش در افناست

فرّاشِ اجل زبهرِ دیگر منزِل

ویران کند این خیمه چو سلطان برخاست

٨٣

خیّام که خیمهاّیِ حکمت میدوخت

در کورهٴ غم فتاد و ذاگاه بسوخت

مقراضِ اجل طنابِ عمرش ببُرید

دلّالِ قضا برایگانش بفروخت

line 3, 'stage,' *i.e.* the grave.

83. C. L. N. A. B. I. J. A play on his name, "tent-maker."

84.

In the sweet spring a grassy bank I sought,
And thither wine, and a fair Houri brought :
　　And, though the people called me graceless
　　　dog,
Gave not to Paradise a second thought !

85.

Sweet is rose-ruddy wine in goblets gay,
And sweet are lute and harp and roundelay :
　　But for the zealot who forswears the cup,
'Tis sweet when he is twenty leagues away !

86.

Life, void of wine, and minstrels with their
　　lutes,
And the soft murmurs of Irákian flutes,
　　Were nothing worth : I scan the world and
　　　see,
Save pleasure, life yields naught but bitter
　　fruits.

---

84   C. L. N. A B I J. *Batai*, a contraction   See Bl.,
Prosody, p 10.   The MSS vary somewhat.

٨۴

در فصلِ بهار با بتِ حور سرشت
یك كوزهء مى اگر بود بر لبِ كشت
هر چند بنزدِ عام بد باشد این
از سگ بترم اگر كنم یادِ بهشت

٨٥

در جامِ طرب بادهء گلرنگ خوشست
با نغمهء عود و نالهء چنگ خوشست
زاهد كه خبر ندارد از جامِ شراب
دور از برِ ما هزار فرسنگ خوشست

٨٦

دورانِ جهان بی مى و ساقى خوش نیست
بی زمزمهء نـای عراقى خوش نیست
هر چند در احوالِ جهان مینـگرم
حاصل همه عشرتست و باقى خوش نیست

<hr>

85. N. The MSS. have a variation of this. Note *Khush*.
86. L. N. See an answer to this in No. 97.

87.

Make haste ! soon must you quit this life below.
And pass the veil, and Allah's secrets know :
  Make haste to take your pleasure while you
    may,
You wot not whence you come, nor whither go.

88.

Depart we must ! what boots it then to be :—
To walk in vain desires eternally ?
  Nay, but if heaven vouchsafe no place of rest,
What power to cease our wanderings have we ?

89.

To chant wine's praises is my daily task,
I live encompassed by cup, bowl and flask ;
  Zealot ! if reason be thy guide, then know
That guide of me doth ofttimes guidance ask.

---

87 C. L N. A I   In line 3 scan *niẻ iniyaz.*
88 N. In line 3 scan *jáyigá* Bl . Prosody. p 15.
89. C. L N. A I J.   In line 1 scan *maddahiyi*. and

٨٧

دریاب که از روح جدا خواهی رفت

در پردهٔ اسرار خدا خواهی رفت

می خور که ندانی از کجا آمدهٔ

خوشباش ندانی که کجا خواهی رفت

٨٨

رفتن چو حقیقتست پس بودن چیست

راهِ طمعِ محال پیمودن چیست

جائیکه بمصلحت بخواهند گذاشت

فارغ ز سفر بودن و آسودن چیست

٨٩

عمریست که مدّاحیِ می وردِ منست

و اسبابِ میست هر چه در گردِ منست

زاهد اگر استادِ تو عقلست اینجا

خوشباش که استادِ تو شاگردِ منست

---

compare Horace, "*Edocet artes ;*

Fecundi calices quem non fecere disertum."

90.

O men of morals! why do ye defame,

And thus misjudge me?　I am not to blame.

　　Save weakness for the grape, and beauty's
　　　　charms,

What sins of mine can any of ye name?

91.

Who treads in passion's footsteps here below,

A helpless pauper will depart, I trow;

　　Remember who you are, and whence you
　　　　come,

Consider what you do, and whither go.

92.

Skies like a zone our weary lives enclose,

And from our tear-stained eyes an Oxus flows,

　　Hell is a fire enkindled of our griefs;

Heaven but a moment's respite from our woes.

90　C L N A I J.　This change of persons is called
Iltifát　Gladwin, Persian Rhetoric. p 56

91　C l N A l　*Khabarat*·　see Bl, Prosody, p v

٩٠

فاسق خوانند مردمانم پیوست

من بیگنهم خیالِ شان بر من بست

بر من بخلافِ شرع ای اهلِ صلاح

جز خمر و لواطه و زنا جرم نه است

٩١

گر در پیِ شهوت و هوا خواهی رفت

از من خبرت که بینوا خواهی رفت

بنگر چه کسی و از کجا آمده‌ء

میدان که چه میکنی کجا خواهی رفت

٩٢

گردون کمری زعمرِ فرسوده‌ء ماست

جیحون اثری ز چشمِ پالوده‌ء ماست

دوزخ شرری ز رنجِ بیهوده‌ء ماست

فردوس دمی ز وقتِ آسوده‌ء ماست

Line 3, *hasi*, qy. *kiyi*, " who thou art."

92   C. L N A. B I J.   This balanced arrangement of
similes is called *Tusi'a*   Gladwin, p 5

93.

I am an erring slave, accept Thou me !
My soul is dark, make me Thy light to see !
 If heaven be but the wage for service done,
Where are Thy bounty and Thy charity ?

94.

Did He who made me fashion me for hell,
Or destine me for heaven ? I cannot tell.
 Yet will I not renounce cup, lute and love,
Nor earthly cash for heavenly credit sell.

95.

From right and left the censors came and stood,
Saying, "Renounce this wine, this foe of good :"
 But if wine be the foe of holy faith,
By Allah, right it is to drink its blood !

---

93 C L N A I J Arabic words like *jazá*' drop the
hamza in Persian, except with the *izáfat* (Bl , Prosody 14)
For this *hamza*, *ya* is often used, as here

٩٣

من بندهٔ عاصیم رضای تو کجاست
تاریك دلم نور و صفای تو کجاست
مارا تو بهشت اگر بطاعت بخشی
این مزد بود لطف و عطای تو کجاست

٩٤

من هیچ ندانم که مرا آن که سرشت
کرد اهلِ بهشتِ خوب یا دوزخِ زشت
جامی و بتی و بربطی بر لب کشت
این هر سه مرا نقد و ترا نسیه بهشت

٩٥

من می خورم و مخالفان از چپ و راست
گویند مخور باده که دینرا اعداست
چون دانستم که می عدوی دینست
واللّه بخورم خونِ عدو را که رواست

93. Ascribed by T. to Ansari (d. 481 A.H.).

94. C. L. N. A. B. I. In line 4 the *izáfat* is dropped after silent *he*. Bl. Prosody, p. 15.

95. C. L. N. A. B. I. J. See Koran, ii. 187.

96.

The good and evil with man's nature blent,
The weal and woe that Heaven's decrees have
      sent,—
   Impute them not to motions of the skies,—
Skies than thyself ten times more impotent.

97.

Against death's arrows what are bucklers worth?
What all the pomps and riches of the earth?
   When I survey the world, I see no good
But goodness, all beside is nothing worth.

98.

Weak souls, who from the world cannot refrain,
Hold life-long fellowship with ruth and pain.
   Hearts free from worldly cares have store of
      bliss,
The wealth that others gather proves their bane.

---

96   C L N A I. J   Fate is merely the decree of N'lah
For the distinction between *kazi* and *kadar*, see P' *cxs*
jecdicu Historia Arabua p 207

۹٦

نیکی و بدی که در نهادِ بشر است

شادی و غمی که در قضا و قدر است

با چرخ مکن حواله کاندر رهِ عقل

چرخ از تو هزار بار بیچاره‌تر است

۹۷

تیریکه اجل کشد سپرها هیچست

وین محتشمی و سیم و زرها هیچ است

چندانکه بروی کارها در نگرم

نیکست که نیکست دگرها هیچ است

۹۸

هر دل که درو مایهٔ تجرید کم است

بیچاره همه عمر ندیم ندم است

جز خاطرِ فارغ که نشاطی دارد

باقی همه هر چه هست اسبابِ غم است

---

97. N. Possibly written on the margin by some pious reader as an answer to No. 86.

98. L. N. *Tajríd*, see *Gulshan i Ráz*, p. 8, n.

.

99.

He, in whose bosom wisdom's seed is sown,
To waste a single day is never known;
  Either he strives to work great Allah's will,
Or else exalts the cup, and works his own.

100.

When Allah mixed my clay, He knew full well
My future acts, and could each one foretell,
  Without His fiat nothing can I do;
Is it then just to punish me in hell?

101.

Ye, who are wont to drink on common days,
Need not on Friday quit your drinking ways:
  Adopt my creed, and count all days the same,
Be worshippers of God, and not of days.

---

99 C L N A B I J   For *tarabe* in the MSS, I
read *tarafe*, " a portion "

100 C L N A I.   Cowper's lines, slightly altered,
apply to all predestinarians :—

٩٩

هر کو طرفی ز عقل در دل میکاشت
یکروز ز عمرِ خویش ضایع نگذاشت
یا در طلبِ رضایِ یزدان کوشید
یا راحتِ خود گزید و ساغر بر داشت

١٠٠

یزدان چو گلِ وجودِ مارا آراست
دانست ز فعلِ ما چه خواهد بر خاست
بی حکمش نیست هر گناهی که مراست
پس سوختنِ قیامت از بهرِ چه خواست

١٠١

یکهفته شراب خورده باشی پیوست
هان تا ندهی بروزِ آدینه ز دست
در مذهبِ ما شنبه و ادینه یکیست
جبّار پرست باش نه روز پرست

" Ten thousand mortals, drowned in endless woe,
For doing what they were compelled to do."

101. L. N. In line 3 scan *yākīst*.

102.

If grace be grace, and Allah gracious be,
Adam from Paradise why banished He?
  Grace to poor sinners shown is grace indeed;
In grace hard earned by works no grace I see.

103.

Dame Fortune's smiles are full of guile, beware!
Her scimitar is sharp to smite, take care!
  If e'er she drop a sweetmeat in thy mouth,
'Tis poisonous,—to swallow it forbear!

104.

Where ruddy tulips grow and roses red,
Know that a mighty monarch's blood was shed;
  And where the violet rears her purple tuft,
Be sure some black-moled girl doth rest her
      head.

---

102   N   The *tashdíd* of *rabb* is dropped.   Bl, Prosody,
p. iv
  103.   C L A B I.   *Húsh* contracted from *hósh.*

١٠٢

یا رب تو کریمی و کریمی کرم است

عاصی ز چه رو برون ز باغ ارم است

با طاعتم ار ببخشی آن نیست کرم

با معصیتم اگر ببخشی کرم است

١٠٣

هُش دار که روزگار شورانگیزست

ایمن منشین که تیغِ دوران تیزست

در کامِ تو گر زمانه لوزینه دهد

زنهار فرو مبر که زهرٌ آمیزست

١٠۴

هر جا که گلی و لاله زاری بودست

از سرخیِ خونِ شهریاری بودست

هر برگِ بنفشه کز زمین می روئید

خالیست که بر رخِ نگاری بودست

104   A. B L   The MSS. have a variation of this, beginning *Har khisht hi.*

105.

Wine is a melting ruby, cup the mine ;
Cup is the body, and the soul is wine ,

    These crystal goblets smile with ruddy wine
Like tears, that blood of wounded hearts
        enshrine.

106.

Drink wine ! 'tis life etern, and travail's meed,
Fruitage of youth, and balm of age's need ;

    'Tis the glad time of roses, wine and friends ;
Rejoice thy spirit—that is life indeed.

107.

Drink wine ! long must you sleep within the
        tomb,
Without a friend, or wife to cheer your gloom ;

   Hear what I say, and tell it not again,
" Never again can withered tulips bloom."

---

105. L B
106. L. B. There being no izáfat after yárdu, sar i

۱۰۵

می لعلِ مذاب ست و صراحی کانست
جسمست پیاله و شرابش جانست
آن جامِ بلورین که ز می خندانست
اشکی ست که خونِ دل در و پنهانست

۱۰٦

می نوش که عمرِ جاودانی اینست
خود حاصل از دورِ جوانی اینست
هنگامِ گل است و مل و یاران سرِمست
خوش باش دمی که زندگانی اینست

۱۰۷

می خور که بزیرِ گل بسی خواهی خفت
بی مونس و بی حریف و بی و همدم و جفت
زنهار بکس مگو تو این رازِ نهفت
هر لالهٴ پژمرده نخواهد بشگفت

---

mast must agree with *hangám*, or be predicate to *yárán*.
107. C. A. B. I. J.

108.

They preach how sweet those Houri brides
     will be,
But I say wine is sweeter—taste and see!
   Hold fast this cash, and let that credit go,
And shun the din of empty drums like me.

109.

Once and again my soul did me implore,
To teach her, if I might, the mystic lore ;
   I bade her *Alif* learn and naught beside.
Who knows that letter well need learn no more.

110.

I came not hither of my own freewill,
And go against my wish, a puppet still ;
   Cupbearer! gird thy loins, and fetch some
     wine ;
To purge the world's despite, my goblet fill.

---

108. C L A B I J. *Súi*, "nuptials."
109. B *Alif kafat*, the One (God) is enough Probably a quotation. Hafiz (Ode 416) uses the same expres-

١٠٨

گویند مرا چو سور با حور خوش است
من می گویم که آبِ انگور خوش است
این نقد بگیر و دست ازان نسیه بدار
کاوازِ دهل شنیدن از دور خوش است

١٠٩

دل گفت مرا علمِ لدنّی هوس است
تعلیم بکن اگر ترا دست رس است
گفتم که الف گفتَ دگر هیچ مگو
در خانه اگر کس است یك حرف بس است

١١٠

چون آمدنم بمن نبُد روزِ نخست
وین رفتن بیمرادِ عزمیست درست
بر خیز و میان به بند ای ساقی چست
کاندوهِ جهان بمی فرو خواهم شست

---

sion: "He who knows the One knows all." *Kafat* in the
MS. may be read *guft.*

110. C. L. A. B. I. J. *'azmé, yá i tankír,* or *tausifi?*
See note to No. 373.

111.

How long must I make bricks upon the sea?
Beshrew this vain task of idolatry ;
   Call not Khayyám a denizen of hell ;
One while in heaven, and one in hell is he.

112.

Sweet is the breath of Spring to rose's face,
And thy sweet face adds charm to this fair place ;
   To-day is sweet, but yesterday is sad,
And sad all mention of its parted grace.

113.

Arise and give me wine ! From speech forbear,
To-night thy lips shall be my only fare :
   Give me some wine as ruddy as thy cheeks,
My good resolves are loosened like thy hair.

---

111   C. L. A. B I J.   *Andar-ba*, Bl, Prosody, 12.
112.   C. L A. B I. J.   *Khush* is pronounced *khash* or
khush. Bl, Prosody. p. 12   *Gáyí* is generally written with

١١١

تا چند زنم بروي درياها خشت

بيزار شدم ز بت پرستانِ كنشت

خيّام كه گفت دوزخى خواهد بود

كه رفت بدوزخ و كه اندر به بهشت

١١٢

بر چهرهٔ گل نسيمِ نو روز خوشست

در صحنِ چمن رويِ دل افروز خوشست

از دى كه گذشت هر چه گوئى خوش نيست

خوش باش و ز دى مگو كه امروز خوشست

١١٣

بر خيز و بده باده چه جاي سخنست

كامشب دهنِ تنگكِ تو روزيِّ من است

ما را چو رخِ خويش مى گلگون ده

كين توبتِ من چو زلفِ تو پر شكنست

_____

hamza on the first *ya*, but in some MSS. *fatha* is substituted for the *hamza* [?].

113. B. *Rôziyyî*. See note to No. 28.

114.

At first I sought Pen, Tablet, Heaven and Hell
Beyond the skies where sun and planets dwell,
But then the master sage instructed me,
" Seek in thyself Pen, Tablet, Heaven and Hell."

115.

The fruit of certitude *he* cannot pluck,
The path that leads thereto who never struck,
Nor ever shook the bough with strenuous
hand ;
To-day is lost ; hope for to-morrow's luck.

116.

Now Spring to joyance doth the world invite,
And quick hearts wend afield in keen delight.
In every breeze there whispers 'Isa's breath,
Each bough puts forth a Musa's hand of white.

114. B L *I e* they have a merely subjective existence
Allah writes his decrees on the " tablet " with the " pen "
Koran, lxviii. 1
115. L. B *Lit* " Consider to-morrow your fir l y "

١١۴

برتر ز سپهرِ خاطرم روزِ نخست
لوح و قلم و بهشت و دوزخ می جست
پس گفت مرا معلّم از رایِ درست
لوح و قلم و بهشت و دوزخ با تُست

١١۵

آنرا که برِ نهالِ تحقیق نرُست
زانست که او نیست درین راه درست
هرکس زده است دست در شاخی سست
امروز چو دی شناس و فردا چو نخست

١١۶

اکنون که جهانرا بخوشی دست رسیست
هر زنده دلی را سویِ صحرا هوسیست
بر هر شاخی طلوعِ موسیا دستیست
در هر نفسی خروشِ عیسیا نفسیست

116. B. Alluding to the life-giving breath of Jesus,
and the white hand of Moses. (Exodus iv. 6.) *Bakhashi
dustrase (yá i tankir)*, "an aider to joy," *i.e.* Spring.

117.

Alas for that cold heart, which never glows
With love, nor e'er that charming sadness
          knows;
   The days misspent with no redeeming love;—
No days are wasted half as much as those!

118.

The zephyrs waft thy fragrance, and it takes
My heart, and me, his master, he forsakes;
   Careless of me he pants and leaps to thee.
And thee his pattern and ensample makes!

119.

Drink wine! and then as Mahmud thou wilt
          reign,
And hear a music passing David's strain:
   Think not of past or future, seize to-day.
Then all thy life will not be lived in vain.

---

117   Bl L B. Note *wa* omitted in line 2, Bl B reads
dilfirözi, which does not scan *Saudāzādāī mihr* = struck
melancholy by love
   118   Bl C. L. A I J. Ascribed to Abu Saʻid (S Lith,
No. 43). C. writes *buyi* with two *yás*. and *hamza* on

١١٧

ای وای بران دل که درو سوزی نیست

سودازده‌ء مهرِ دلافروزی نیست

روزی که تو بی عشق بسر خواهی برد

ضایع‌تر از ان روز ترا روزی نیست

١١٨

از بادِ صبا دلم چو بويِ تو گرفت

مارا بگذاشت جست و جويِ تو گرفت

اکنون ز منش هیچ نمی آید یاد

بويِ تو گرفته بود و خويِ تو گرفت

١١٩

با باده نشین که ملك محمود این است

وز چنگ شنو که لَحَنِ دأود این است

از آمده و رفته دگر یاد مکن

حالی خوش باش زانکه مقصود این است

the first. The second *yá* seems to be *yá i batni* or *tansifi*,
though that is usual only before adjectives. Bl., Prosody,
p. 11.

119. Bl. C. L. A. I. J. Mahmud, the celebrated king
of Ghazna.

120.

Ten Powers, nine spheres, and twice four
    heavens made He,
Seven planets, of six aspects, as we see,
    Five senses, and four elements, three souls,
Two worlds, but only one, O man, like thee.

121.

Jewry hath seen a thousand 'Isas die,
Sinai a thousand Musas mount the sky;
    How many Cæsars Rome's proud forum
    crossed!
'Neath Kasra's dome how many monarchs lie!

122.

Gold breeds not wit, but to wit lacking bread
Earth's flowery carpet seems a dungeon bed:
    'Tis his full purse that makes the rose to smile,
While empty-handed violets hang the head.

120 L A summary of the Muhammadan doctrine
of "Emanations" See *Gulshan i Raz* p 21. Three souls,
i e vegetive, animal and human as in Aristotle's *De
Anima*. *Akhtaram* (?) also in Cambridge MS

۱۲۰

ده عقل و ز دهُ رواق وز هشت بهشت

هفت اخترم از شش جهت این نامه نوشت

کز پنج حواس و چار ارکان و سه روح

ایزد بدو عالم چو تو یك كس نسرشت

۱۲۱

دیریست که صد هزار عیسیٰ دیدست

طوریست که صد هزار موسیٰ دیدست

قصّریست که صد هزار قیصر بگذشت

طاقیست که صد هزار کسریٰ دیدست

۱۲۲

سیم ارچه نه مایهٔ خردمندانست

بی سیمان را باغ جهان زندانست

از دست تهی بنفشه سر بر زانوست

وز کیسهٔ زر دهان گل خندانست

---

121. L. J. Time is long and life short.

122. L. Alluding to the golden stamens of the rose.
I supply *tihi* from the Cambridge MS.

123

Heaven's cruel wheel much righteous blood
    doth shed,
And strike down roses on their garden bed ;
  Plume thee not on thy youth and looks,
    my son !
Full many a bud is blasted ere 'tis spread.

124.

What lord is fit to rule but " Truth " ? not one.
What creatures disobey His rule ? not one.
  All things that are are such as He decrees,
And naught is there beside beneath the sun

125.

That azure coloured vault, and golden tray
Have turned, and will turn yet for many a day:
  And just so we, impelled by turns of fate,—
We come here for a while, then pass away.

---

123   L. In line 3 scan *jur inīyay*
124   C. L. A I. " The Truth " is the Sufi name for
the Deity. Note *tashdīd* on *Hakk* dropped

١٢٣

بس خونِ كسان كه چرخِ بيباك بريخت
بس گل كه بر آمد از گِل و پاك بريخت
بر حسن و جوانی ای پسر غرّه مشو
بس غنچهٴ ناشگفته بر خاك بريخت

١٢٤

جز حق حَكَمی كه حكّم را شايد نيست
دستی كه ز حكمِ او برون آيد نيست
هر چيز كه هست آنچنان ميبايد
آنچيز كه آنچنان نمی بايد نيست

١٢٥

اين گمبدِ لاجوردی و زرّينِ طشت
بسيار بگشتنست و دگر خواهد گشت
يكچند ز اقتضایِ دورانِ قضا
ما نيز چو ديگران رسيديم و گذشت

---

125 Bl L *Guzasht* "It is all over with us" Bl.
"Golden tray," the Sun. In line 1 scan *lájuardiyó* Bl,
Prosody, p 11.

126.

Since 'twas the Master did these creatures
    frame,
Why doth he cast them to disgrace and shame?
    If they be formed aright, why doth he crush
       them?
And if awry, to whom belongs the blame?

127.

Kindness to friends and foes 'tis well to show,
No kindly heart can prove unkind, I trow:
    Harshness will alienate a bosom friend,
And kindness reconcile a deadly foe.

128.

To lover true, what matters dark or fair?
Or if the loved one silk or sackcloth wear,
    Or he on down or dust, or rise to heaven?
Yea, though she sink to hell, he'll seek her there.

---

126 C L A I J Also in *Musad al-'Ibâd* (Journal
R A S. xxx p 362) which for *tab'iyi* reads *tab'ydi'* (an
obvious misprint) and other variants. Sukar, Arab

۱۲۶

دارنده چو ترکیبِ طبائع آراست

از بهرِ چه او فکندش اندر کم و کاست

گر نیک آمد شکستن از بهرِ چه بود

ور نیک نیامد این صُوَر عیب کراست

۱۲۷

با دشمنِ و دوست فعلِ نیکو نیکوست

بد کی کند آنکه نیکیش عادت و خوست

با دوست چو بد کنی شود دشمنِ تو

با دشمن اگر نیک کنی گردد دوست

۱۲۸

در چشمِ محققان چه زیبا چه زشت

منزلگهِ عاشقان چه دوزخ چه بهشت

پوشیدنِ بیدلان چه اطلس چه پلاس

زیرِ سرِ عاشقان چه بالین چه خشت

---

plural of *súrat*.

127.   L.   In line 2 scan *néykiyash*.

128.   L.   Probably mystical.

129.

Full many a hill and vale I journeyed o'er;
Journeyed around the wide world's quarters
        four,
   But never heard of pilgrim who returned;
When once they go, they go to come no more.

130.

Wine-houses flourish through this thirst of mine.
Loads of remorse weigh down this back of mine;
   Yet, if I sinned not, what would mercy do?
Mercy is fostered by these sins of mine.

131.

Thy being is the being of Another,
Thy passion is the passion of Another.
   Cover thy head, and think, and thou wilt see,
Thy hand is but the cover of Another.

---

129   C L N (in part) A I. J.
130.   C. Bl L. A I. J. Bl. quotes similar sentiments
from Nizámi and Háfiz, viz Sin, that grace may abound.

١٢٩

بسیار بگشتیم بگردِ در و دشت

اندر همه آفاقِ بگشتیم بگشت

از کس نشنیدیم که آمد زین راه

راهی که برفت راه رو باز نگشت

١٣٠

آبادِ خرابات ز می خوردنِ ماست

خونِ دو هزار توبه در گردنِ ماست

گر من نکنم گناه رحمت که کند

رحمت همه موقوفِ گنه کردنِ ماست

١٣١

این هستیِ تو هستیِ هستیِ دگرست

وین مستیِ تو مستیِ مستیِ دگرست

رو سر بگریبانِ تفکّر در کش

کین دستِ تو آستینِ دستیِ دگرست

---

131. Bl. Meaning, God is the *Fáʼil i haqíqí*, the only
real agent. *Hastí digar*—another being—*hast*, with *yá*
batní.

132.

From learning to the cup your bridle turn;
All lore of world to come, save Kausar, spurn;
 Your turban pawn for wine, or keep a shred
To bind your brow, and all the remnant burn

133.

See! from the world what profit have I gained?
What fruitage of my life in hand retained?
 What use is Jamshed's goblet, once 'tis
  crushed?
What pleasure's torch, when once its light has
 waned?

134.

When life is spent, what's Balkh or Nishapore?
What sweet or bitter, when the cup runs o'er?
 Come drunk! full many a moon will wax and
  wane
In times to come, when we are here no more.

---

132 N The metre shows we must pronounce *tarafe,*
"a portion," not *tarfe,* "a girdle." *Kausar,* the river of
wine in Paradise

١٣٢

از فضلِ عنان بهپیچ و در ساغر پیچ
از خلد و سقر بگُذر و در کوثر پیچ
دستارِ قصب ببادهٔ بفُروش ومترس
کم کَن قصبی پس طرفی بر سر پیچ

١٣٣

بنْگر ز جهان چه طرْف بر بستم هیچ
وز حاصلِ عمر چیست در دستم هیچ
شمْعِ طربم ولی چو بنْشستم هیچ
من جامِ جم ولی چو بشکستم هیچ

١٣۴

چون جان بلب آمد چه نشاپور وچه بلخ
پیماذه، چو پُر شود چه شیرین و چه تلخ
می نوش که بعد از من و تو ماهِ بسی
از سلخ بغرّه آید از غرّه بسلخ

---

133. L. N. *Tarf bar bastan*, "to reap advantage."
Ascribed to Khaqáni, d. 595 A.H.
134. C, L, N, A, B, I, J, H.

135.

O fair ! whose cheeks checkmate red eglantine.
And draw the game with those fair maids of
    Chín ;
  You played one glance against the king of
    Babil
And took his pawns, and knights, and rooks.
    and queen.

136.

Life's caravan is hastening on its way ;
Brood not on troubles of the coming day.
  But fill the wine-cup, ere sweet night be gone.
And snatch a pleasant moment while you may.

137.

He, who the world's foundations erst did lay,
Doth bruise full many a bosom day by day,
  And many a ruby lip and musky tress
Doth coffin in the earth, and shroud with clay.

---

135 L B
136 C. L N. A. B. I J

١٣٥

اى عارضِ تو نهاده بر نسرين طرح
روىِ تو فكنده بر بتانِ چين طرح
دى غمزهء تو داده شهِ بابل را
اسب و رخ و فيل و بيذق و فرزين طرح

١٣٦

اين قافلهء عمر عجب ميگذرد
درياب دمى كه از طرب ميگذرد
ساقى غمِ فرداىِ حريفان چه خورى
پيش آر پياله را كه شب ميگذرد

١٣٧

آنكس كه زمين و چرخ و افلاك نهاد
بس داغ كه او بر دلِ غمناك نهاد
بسيار لبِ چو لعل وزلفينِ چو مشك
در طبلِ زمين و حقّهٔ خاك نهاد

---

137 C L N A I J So Job, " Is it good unto thee
that thou shouldest oppress. that thou shouldest despise the
work of thine hands ? ' x. 3

138.

Be not entrapped by world's insidious wiles :
O foolish ones, ye know her tricks and guiles ;
   Your precious lifetime cast not to the winds .
Get store of wine, and court a sweetheart's
      smiles.

139.

Comrades ! I pray you, physic me with wine,
Make this wan amber face like rubies shine.
   And, if I die, use wine to wash my corpse,
And lay me in a coffin made of vine !

140

When Allah yoked the coursers of the sun,
And launched the Pleiades their race to run,
   My lot was fixed in fate's high chancery :
Then why blame me for wrong that fate has
      done ?

---

138. N

139   C L N. A B L. *Kahrubá*, "amber " literally
"attractor of straw." *Ráy* i—*isijat* before the epithet
Lumsden, ii 259.

١٣٨

ای بیخبران عشوهٔ دنیا مخرید
چون از همه حالهای او با خبرید
و این عمر عزیز خویش مدّهید بباد
هان یار طلب کنید و هین باده خورید

١٣٩

ای همنفسان مرا ز می قوت کنید
وین روی چو کهربا چو یاقوت کنید
چون مرده شوم بمی بشوئید مرا
وز چوب رزم تختهٔ تابوت کنید

١٤٠

آنروز که توسن فلك زین کردند
وارایش مشتری و پروین کردند
این بود نصیب ما ز دیوان قضا
مارا چه گنه قسمت ما این کردند

140 C L N A I J Also ascribed in A K to Afzal Kashi, d 707 A H Mushtāriyyŏ, see Bl, Prosody, p 11. In line 3 some MSS read mai for in. See No. 144.

141.

Ah! seasoned wine oft falls to rawest fools,
And clumsiest workmen own the finest tools;
    And Turki maids, fit to delight men's hearts,
Lavish their smiles on beardless boys in schools!

142.

Whilom, ere youth's conceit had waned, me-
        thought
Answers to all life's problems I had wrought:
    But now, grown old and wise, too late I see
My life is spent, and all my lore is naught.

143.

Fools, who of prayer-mats make such great
        display,
To vain hypocrisy a tribute pay:
    Strange! under cover of this saintly show
They live like heathen, and the faith betray.

---

141.   N   So Hafiz, " If that Turki maid of Shiraz,' &c.
142.   N. [C. A and I give another version of this
143.   C L N A I   In line 2, note the arrangement of

١٤١

افسوس که نانِ پخته خامان دارند

اسبابِ تمام ناتمامان دارند

چشمِ خوشِ ترکان بتماشایِ دلست

ملکیست که شاگرد و غلامان دارند

١٤٢

اکنون که دم ز عمر محروم نشد

کم بود ز اسرار که مفهوم نشد

چون نیك همی بنگرم از رویِ خرد

عمرم بگذشت و هیچ معلوم نشد

١٤٣

آنقوم که سجّاده پرستند خرند

زیرا که بزیرِ بارِ سالوس درند

وین از همه طرفه ترکه در پردهٔ زهّد

اسلام فروشند و ز کافر بترند

---

the prepositions *ba* .... *dar*, Bl., Prosody, 13. There is
a proverb, "The Devil lives in Mecca and Medinah."
See also Burckhardt, Arabic Proverbs, No. 480.

144.

To him, who would his sins extenuate,
Let pious men this verse reiterate,
  "To call God's pre-cience the cause of sin
In wisdom's purview is but folly's prate."

145.

He brought me hither, to my great surprise;
From life I gather but a dark surmise;
  I go perforce. Why come? Why live?
    Why go?
I ask these questions, but find no replies.

146.

When I recall my grievous sins to mind,
Fire burns my breast, and tears my vision blind,
  Yet, when a slave repents, is it not meet
His lord should pardon, and again be kind?

---

144 L N *Sahl*, "of no account" Probably a gloss
Ascribed in the Táríkh i Guzída to Izz ud Din Karaji
(Journ R A S, xxxiii p. 3)
  115 C L N, A. I read *iztarâb*, "perplexity," with

۱۴۴

آنكس كه گنه بنزدِ او سهل بَوَد
اين ذكته بگویَد انكه او اهَل بَوَد
علمِ ازلی علّتِ عصیان کردن
نزدیكِ حكیم غایتِ جُهل بَوَد

۱۴٥

آورد باضطرابم اوّل بوجود
جز حیرتم از حیات چیزی نفزود
رفتیم باکراه و ندانیم چه بود
زین آمدن و رفتن و بودن مقصود

۱۴٦

اندیشهٔ جرمم چو بخاطر گذرد
از آتشِ سینه آبم از سر گذرد
لیكن شرطست بنده چون توبه كند
مخدوم بلطفِ خویش از سر گذرد

L. and N. Query *iztarár*, "compulsion."

146. L. N. In line 2, *az sar guzarad* means "issues from the head (eyes)," and in line 4, "remits the penalty." This change of meaning is called *Tajnis*.

147.

They at whose lore the world doth stand
    amazed,

Whose high thoughts, like Borák, to heaven are
    raised,

  Strive to know Thee in vain, and like heaven's
    wheel

Their heads are turning, and their brains are
    dazed.

148.

Allah hath promised wine in Paradise,

Why then is wine on earth declared a vice?

  An Arab once did Hamza's camel hough,—

That's why the Prophet's ban is so precise.

149.

Now of old joys naught but the name is left.

Of all old friends but wine we are bereft.

  And that wine *new*; but still cleave to the cup,

For save the cup, what solace is there left?

---

147. C. L N. A   Borák, the steed on which Muhammad made his famous nocturnal ascent to heaven

148   L N. According to the common story, it was

۱۴۷

آنها که خلاصهٔ جهان ایشانند
بر اوجِ فلك براقِ فكرت رانند
در معرفتِ ذاتِ تو مانند فلك
سرگشته و سر نگون و سر گردانند

۱۴۸

ایزد ببهشت وعده با ما مَی کرد
پس در دو جهان حرام میرا كی کرد
شخصی ز عرب ناقهٔ حمزه پی کرد
پیغمبرِ ما حرام می بروی کرد

۱۴۹

اکنون که ز خوشدلی بجز نام نماند
یك همدمِ پخته جز مَی خام نماند
دستِ طرب از ساغرِ می باز مگیر
امروز که در دست بجز جام نماند

Hamza who got drunk and houghed 'Ali's camel. L. reads
khamra, "drink," but does not clear up the difficulty.

149. L. N. B. In line 2 scan *māyī*.

150.

The world will last long after my poor fame
Has passed away, yea, and my very name.

    Aforetime, ere we came, we were not missed:
When we are dead and gone, 'twill be the same.

151.

The sages who have compassed sea and land,
Their secret to search out, and understand,—

    My mind misgives me if they ever solve
The scheme on which this universe is planned.

152.

Ah! wealth takes wings, and leaves our hands
      all bare,
And death's rough hands delight our hearts to
      tear;

    And from the nether world let none escape,
To bring us tidings of the pilgrims there.

---

150   N   The contraction *bŭd* for *bŭd* is archaic. Bl,
Prosody, 13   " Il n'y a pas d'homme nécessaire."
    151.   C L N A. I.

١٥٠

ای بس که نباشیم و جهان خواهد بود
نی نام زما و نی نشان خواهد بود
زین پیش نبودیم و نبُد هیچ خلل
زین پس چو نباشیم و همان خواهد بود

١٥١

آنها که جهان زیرِ قدم فرسودند
و اندر طلبش هر دو جهان پیمودند
آگاه نمیشوم که ایشان هرگز
زین حال چنانکه هست آگه بودند

١٥٢

افسوس که سرمایه زکف بیرون شد
وز دستِ اجل بسی جگرها خون شد
کس نامَد از آنجهان که پرسم از وی
کاحوالِ مسافرانِ عالم چون شد

152. C. L. N. A. I. In line 3 the *Alif* in *az wé* is not
treated as an *Alif i wasl*, hence *sam*, the syllable preceding
it, is long.

153.

Strange! the great lord, the wealthy citizen
Find their own lives a burden sore, but when
    They meet with poorer men, not slaves to
        sense,
They scarcely deign to reckon them as men.

154.

The wheel of heaven, still busied with despite,
Will ne'er unloose a wretch from grievous plight;
    But when it lights upon a smitten heart,
Straightway prepares another blow to smite.

155.

Now is the volume of my youth outworn,
My happy spring by autumn overborne:
    Ah, bird of youth! I marked not when you
        came,
Nor when you fled, and left me thus forlorn.

---

153   C. L. N. A. I   In line 1 scan *Ádámíshá*   See
Bl. Prosody, p. xii Section xxix
   154.   C L. N. A. I.—Note *ra* separated from its noun

١٥٣

این جمع اکابر که مناصب دارند

از غصّه و غم ز جانِ خود بیزارند

و آنکس که اسیرِ حرص چون ایشان نیست

وین طرفه که آدمیش می نشمارند

١٥٤

این چرخِ جفاپیشهٔ عالی بنیاد

هرگز گرهِ کارِ کسی را نکشاد

هرجا که دلی دید که داغی دارد

داغِ دگری بر سرِ آن داغ نهاد

١٥٥

افسوس که نامهٔ جوانی طی شد

وین تازه بهارِ شادمانی طی شد

آن مرغِ طرب که نام او بود شباب

فریاد ندانم که کی آمد کی شد

---

by intervening genitives. Vullers, Section 207.

155. C. L N A I. In line 4 scan *kăyámad*, dissolving
the diphthong.

156.

These fools, by dint of ignorance most crass,
Think they in wisdom all mankind surpass ;
   And glibly do they damn as infidel,
Each one who is not, like themselves, an ass.

157.

Still be the tavern thronged with joyful choir,
And Pharisaic skirts consumed with fire ;
   Still be those tattered frocks, and azure robes
Trod under feet of revellers in the mire.

158.

Why toil ye to ensue illusions vain,
And good, or maybe evil, thence attain ?
   Were ye the Zamzam, or the fount of life,
In the earth's breast, like them, ye'd sink again.

---

156. N Also ascribed to Avicena of Balkh (d 427 A H).
Ethé Avicena, No 6   So Job, " Ye are the people, and
wisdom shall die with you."

۱۵٦

با این دو سه نادان که جهاندارانند
از جهل که دانای جهان ایشانند
خوشباش که از خرّی ایشان بمثل
هر کو نه خرست کافرش میدانند

۱۵۷

پیوسته خرابات ز رندان خوشباد
در دامن زهد زاهدان آتش باد
آن دلق بصد پاره و آن صوف کبود
افتاده بزیر پای دردی کش باد

۱۵۸

تاچند اسیر رنگ و بو خواهی شد
چند ازپی هر زشت و نکو خواهی شد
گر چشمهٔ زمزمی و گر ز آب حیات
آخر بدل خاک فرو خواهی شد

---

157. C. L. N. A. J. Hafiz (Ode v.) speaks of the blue robes of certain Darvishes, as a mark of hypocrisy.

158. C. L. N. A. I.

159.

Till the Friend pours his wine to glad my heart,
No kisses to my face will heaven impart :
    They say " Repent," but how can I repent,
Ere Allah deigns to soften my hard heart ?

160.

When I am dead, take me and grind me small,
So that I be a warning unto all,
    And knead me into clay with wine, and then
Use me to stop the wine-jar's mouth withal.

161.

What though the sky with its blue canopy
Doth close us in so that we cannot see ; .
    In the etern Cupbearer's wine, methinks,
There float a myriad bubbles like to me.

---

159   C. L. N. A I   Meaning, man is powerless to
mend his ways without Divine grace.
    160.   C. L. N. A. I. J.

۱٥۹

تا یار شراب جانفزایم ندهد

صد بوسه فلك بر سر و پایم ندهد

گویند که توبه کن اگر وقت آید

چون توبه کنم تا که خدایم ندهد

۱٦۰

چون مرده شوم خاك مرا كم سازید

واحوال مرا عبرت مردم سازید

خاك تن من ببادہ آغشته كنید

وز كالبدم خشت سر خم سازید

۱٦۱

خیّام اگرچه خرگه چرخ كبود

زد خیمه و دربست در گفت و شنود

چون شكل حباب بادہ در جام وجود

ساقیّ ازل هزار خیّام نمود

---

161. N. For the *tashdid* on *sákiyyí* in line 4, see Bl.,
Prosody, p. 11, and Lumsden, Grammar, vol. ii., p. 247.

162.

Take heart !   Trouble will last eternally,
While stars keep countless watches in the sky,
    And see your ashes moulded into bricks,
To build the mansions of posterity.

163.

Glad hearts, who seek not notoriety,
Nor flaunt in gold and silken bravery,
    Haunt not this ruined earth like gloomy owls.
But wing their way, Simurgh-like, to the sky.

164.

Wine's power is known to wine-bibbers alone,
To narrow heads and hearts 'tis never shown :
    I blame not them who never felt its force,
For, till they feel it, how can it be known ?

---

162. L N   C. A and I. split this into two. In line 1
note *izáfat* dropped after silent *he*.

۱۶۲

خوشباش که غصّه دیگران خواهد بود
بر چرخ قرانِ اخترانِ خواهد بود
خشتی که ز قالبِ تو خواهند زدن
ایوانِ سرایِ دیگرانِ خواهد بود

۱۶۳

خرّم دلِ آنکسی که معروف نشُد
در جُبّه و درّاعه و در صوف نشد
سیمرغ صفت بعرش پروازی کرد
در کنجِ خرابهٔ جهان بوف نشُد

۱۶۴

حالِ گل و مل بادهپرستان دانند
نه تنگدلان و تنگدستان دانند
از بیخبری بیخبران معذورند
ذوقیست درین شیوه که مستان دانند

163. C. L. N. A. I.
164. C. N. A. I. J.

'

165.

Needs must the tavern-hunter bathe in wine,
For none can make a tarnished name to shine;
  Go! bring me wine, for none can now restore
Its pristine sheen to this soiled robe of mine.

166.

I wasted life in hope, yet gathered not
In all my life of happiness one jot;
  Now my fear is that life may not endure,
Till I have taken vengeance on my lot!

167.

Be very wary in the soul's domain,
And on the world's affairs your lips refrain;
  Be, as it were, sans tongue, sans ear, sans eye,
While tongue, and ears, and eyes you still retain.

---

165. C. L N A. B I. In line 3 scan *mastúríyí* dissolving the letter of prolongation *yá*.

١٦٥

در میکده جز بمی وضو نتّوان کرد

و ان نام که زشت شد نکو نتّوان کرد

می ده که کنون پردهٴ مستوریِ ما

بدّریده چنان شد که رفو نتّوان کرد

١٦٦

دادم بامید روزگاری بر باد

نا بود ز روزگارِ خود روزی شاد

زان میترسم که روزگارم ندهد

چندانکه ز روزگار بسّتانم داد

١٦٧

در عالمِ جان بهوش میباید بُود

در کارِ جهان خموش میباید بود

تا چشم و زبان و گوش بر جا باشد

بیچشم و زبان و گوش میباید بُود

---

166. C. L. N. A I. *Rozgârê*, "some time" In line 3, note the *madd* of ـِ dropped. Bl , Prosody, p 11.

167. L. N.

I

168.

Let him rejoice who has a loaf of bread,
A little nest wherein to lay his head,
 Is slave to none, and no man slaves for him,—
In truth his lot is wondrous well be-tead.

169.

What adds my service to Thy majesty?
Or how can sin of mine dishonour Thee?
 O pardon, then, and punish not; I know
Thou 'rt slow to wrath, and prone to clemency.

170.

Hands, such as mine, that handle bowls of wine,
'Twere shame to book and pulpit to confine,
 Zealot! thou 'rt dry, and I am moist with
  drink,
Yea, far too moist to catch that fire of thine!

---

168 C L X. A. I. Note *ica* omitted
169 C L X A. I.

۱٦۸

در دهرِ هر آن که نیمِ نانی دارد
از بهرِ نشست آشیانی دارد
نه خادمِ کس بود نه مخدومِ کسی
گو شاد بزی که خوش جهانی دارد

۱٦۹

در مُلکِ تو از طاعتِ من هیچ فزود
وز معصیتی که رفت نقصانی بود
بگذار و مگیر چونکه معلومم شد
گیرندهٔ دیرّی و گذارندهٔ زود

۱۷۰

دستِ چو منی که جام و ساغر گیرد
حیفست که او دفتر و منبر گیرد
تو زاهدِ خشکّی و منم فاسقِ تر
آتش نشنیده ام که در تر گیرد

171.

Whoso aspires to gain a rose-cheeked fair,
Sharp pricks from fortune's thorns must learn
      to bear.
  See ! till this comb was cleft by cruel cuts,
It never dared to touch my lady's hair.

172.

May my hand ever grasp the cup, I prayed,
And my heart pant for some fair Houri maid :
  They said, " May Allah aid thee to repent ! "
Repent I could not, e'en with Allah's aid !

173.

I passed away, while men to folly clung,
And of my precious pearls not one was strung ,
  Ah fools ! there died with me a thousand
      truths
Which never have been told and never sung.

---

171. C. L X A I. Lyttleton expresses a similar
sentiment.
  172. C. L X. A B. I J Note the conjunctive pro-

١٧١

در دهر كسى بگلعذارى نرسيد

تا بر دلش از زمانه خارى نرسيد

در شانه نگر كه تا بصد شاخ نشد

دستش بسرِ زلفِ نگارى نرسيد

١٧٢

در دست هميشه آبِ انگورم باد

در سرِ هَوَسِ بتانِ چون حورم باد

گوذيد مرا كه ايزدت توبه دهاد

او خود بدهد من نكنم دُورم باد

١٧٣

رفتيم و ز ما زمانه آشفته بماند

با آنكه ز صد گهر يكى سفته نماند

افسوس كه صد هزار معنىِّ دقيق

از بيخردىِّ خلق نا گفته بماند

---

noun *am* separated from its noun, Bl., Prosody, p. xiii.
ū khwud bidihad, "even though he gave it."

173. C. L. N. A. I. For the *tashdīds* on *ma'niyyi* and
bekhiradiyyi, see Bl., Prosody, p. 11.

174.

To-day how sweetly breathes the temperate air,
The rains have newly laved the parched par-
        terre ;
   And bulbuls cry in notes of ecstasy,
" Thou too, O pallid rose, our wine must share ! "

175.

Ere sorrows' inroads make resistance vain,
Bid them with rosy wine your strength sustain :
   You are not gold ; once hidden in the earth,
No one will care to dig you up again !

176.

My coming brought no profit to the sky.
Nor does my going swell its majesty :
   Coming and going put me to a stand,
Ear never heard their wherefore or their why.

174   L N B   Note *khward* rhyming with *guid*   Bl ,
Prosody, p 12   The *rain*, of course, does not count
175.   C. L N A B I. J   Note the old form of the
imperative, *farmiy*.   Bl , Prosody, p 13

١٧۴

روزِبست خوش و هوا نه گرمست ونه سرد

ابر از رخِ گلزار همی شوید گرد

بلبل بزبانِ حالِ ما با گلِ زرد

فریاد همی زند که مَی باید خورد

١٧۵

زان پیش که غمهاتِ شبیخون آرند

فرمای که تا بادهٔ گلگون آرند

تو زر نهٔ ای غافلِ نادان که ترا

در خاك نهند و باز بیرون آرند

١٧٦

از آمدنم نبود گردونرا سُود

وز رفتنِ مَن جاه و جلالش نفزود

ور هیچکسی نیز دو گوشم نشنود

کین آمدن و رفتنم از بهرِ چه بُود

---

176 C. L. N. A. B I. J In line 4 read *ámadan* for
ámadanam, which will not scan Voltaire has some similar
lines in his poem on the Lisbon earthquake.

177.

The heavenly Sage, whose wit exceeds compare,
Counteth each vein, and numbereth every hair:
    Men you may cheat by hypocritic arts,
But how cheat Him to whom all hearts are bare?

178.

Ah! wine lends wings to many a weary wight.
And beauty spots to ladies' faces bright:
    All Ramazan I have not drunk a drop,
Thrice welcome then, O Bairam's blessed night!

179.

All night from maddening thought no rest I get,
With tear-drops big as pearls my breast is wet;
    This head can never take its fill of grief,
How can a bowl be filled while 'tis upset?

---

177   C L N. A I J.

178. C L N A I   Bairam, the feast on the 1st

۱۷۷

سرّت همه داناﻯ فلك ميداند
كو موﻯ بموﻯ ورگﻚ برگﻚ ميداند
گيرم كه بزرق خلقرا بفريبى
با او چه كنى كه يك بيك ميداند

۱۷۸

سودازده‌را باده پر و بال بُوَد
مى بر رخِ خاتون خرد و خال بُوَد
ماه رمضان باده نخورديم و برفت
بارﻯ شبِ عيدِ ماهِ شوّال بُوَد

۱۷۹

شب نيست كه عقل در تحيّر نشود
وز گريه كنارِ من پر از دُر نشود
پر مى نشود كاسهء سر از سودا
هر كاسه كه سر نگون بُوَد پر نشود

<hr>

Shawwal, after Ramazan. In line 2, *khirad* seems wrong, the rhyme would suggest *khar o?*

179. C. L. N. A. I. Note *tashdíd* of *durr* dropped.

180.

To prayer and fasting when I gave my mind,
My soul's desire to compass I designed,

Alas! one sip of wine annulled my fast,
And my ablutions one chance puff of wind!

181

I worship rose-red cheeks with heart and soul,
I suffer not my hand to quit the bowl,

I make each part of me his function do,
Or e'er my parts be swallowed in the Whole.

182.

Love only surface deep is counterfeit,
And, like a half-spent blaze, lacks light and heat;

True love is his, who for long months and
years

Rests not, nor sleeps, nor craves for drink or
meat.

---

180 C L N A I In line 2, scan *kulliyam* In line
4, note *izájat* dropped after silent *he*, For the trifles which
nullify ablutions, see Mishcat ul Masabih, by Matthews,
p 77

۱۸۰

طبعم بنماز و روزه چون مائل شد
گفتم که مرادِ کلّیم حاصل شد
افسوس که آن وضوبِبادی بشکست
وان روزه به نیمِ جرعه می باطل شد

۱۸۱

طبعم همه با رویِ چو گل پیوندد
دستم همه با ساغرِ مل پیوندد
از هر جزوی نصیبِ خود بر دارم
زان پیش که جزویم بکل پیوندد

۱۸۲

عشقی که مجازی بود آبش نبود
چون آتشِ نیمِ مرده تابش نبود
عاشق باید که ماه و سال و شب و روز
آرام و قرار و خورد و خوابش نبود

---

181. C L N A I. Line 4 alludes to reabsorption in
the Divine essence. Note *juzwíyam*, and *tashdíd* of *kull*
dropped

182 L. N B Line 3 is in metre 17.

183.

Why spend life in self-worship, and essay
All Being and Not-being to survey?
 Since Death is ever pressing at your heels,
'Tis best to drink or dream your life away.

184.

Some, filled with overweening phantasy,
Houris in Paradise expect to see;
 But, when the veil is lifted, they will find
How far they are from Thee, how far from Thee!

185.

In Paradise are Houris, as men trow,
And fountains with pure wine and honey flow;
 If these be lawful in the world to come,
May I not love the like down here below?

---

183   C L. N A. I J   In line 2, scan *pāyī*   Being,
i e. the Deity, the only real existence, and Not-being, the

١٨٣

عمرت تا کی بخود پرستی گذرد

یا درپَیِ نیستیّ و هستی گذرد

می نوش که عمری که اجل درپَیِ اوست

آن به که بخواب یا بمستی گذرد

١٨٤

قومی ز گزاف در غرور افتادند

و اندر طلبِ حور و قصور افتادند

معلوم شود چو پردها بر دارند

کز کویِ تو دور و دور و دور افتادند

١٨٥

گویند بهشت و حور و عین خواهد بود

وانجا میِ ناب و انگبین خواهد بود

گر ما می و معشوقه پرستدیم رواست

چون عاقبتِ کار همین خواهد بود

---

nonentity in which His attributes are reflected. See
Gulshan i Ráz, p. 14.

184. C. L. N. A I.   185 C L N. A I. J.

186.

A draught of wine would make a mountain
        dance,
Base is the churl who looks at wine askance;
    Wine is a soul our bodies to inspire,
A truce to this vain talk of temperance!

187.

Oft doth my soul her prisoned state bemoan,
And from her fleshly cage would oft have flown,
    Had not the stirrup of the sacred law
Upborne her foot from dashing on the stone!

188.

The moon of Ramazan is risen, see!
Alas, our wine must henceforth banished be:
    Well! on Sha'bán's last day I'll drink enough
To keep me drunk till Bairam's jubilee.

---

186. C L. N A. I
187   N   Meaning, 'I would make away with myself,
were it not for "the Almighty's canon 'gainst self-slaughter."'

١٨٦

گر باده بكوه بر زنی رقص كند

ناقص بود آنكه باده را نقص كند

از باده مرا توبه چه ميفرمائی

روحيست كه او تربيتِ شخص كند

١٨٧

گه گه، دلِ من درين قفس تنگ آید

از همرهی آب و گلش تنگ آید

گفتم كه مگر بشكنم این زندانرا

پایم ز ركابِ شرع بر سنگ آید

١٨٨

گویند كه ماهِ رمضان گشت پدید

من بعد بگردِ باده نتوان گردید

در آخرِ شعبان بخورم چندان می

كاندر رمضان مست بيفتم تا عيد

---

188. C. L. N. A. I. Note *wa* omitted in line 2. Also
ascribed to Jalal 'Azud Yazdi (d. 793 A.H.). M.

189.

From life we draw now wine, now dregs to
  drink,
Now flaunt in silk, and now in tatters shrunk;
  Such changes wisdom holds of slight account
To those who stand on death's appalling brink !

190.

What sage the eternal secrets e'er unravelled,
Or one short step beyond his nature travelled ?
  From pupils to the masters turn your eyes,
And see, each mother's son alike is gravelled.

191.

Love the world less if thou would'st live in
  peace,
From thrall to fortune's changes get release ;
  Take heart !   The courses of the circling
  heavens
Are not eternal, but ere long will cease.

---

189.   N

190   C. L. N. A. B. I   In line 1. note *i* put after the
genitive following its noun.   *Ijz* .. " impotence is in the

١٨٩

گه شربتِ عیش صاف باشد گه دُرد

گه پوششِ ما پلاش باشد گه بُرد

اینها همه سهل است بنزدِ عاقل

این واقعه سهّلست که میباید مُرد

١٩٠

کس مشکلِ اسرارِ ازلرا نگشاد

کس یکقدم از نهاد بیرون ننهاد

من مینگرم ز مبتدی تا استاد

عجز است بدستِ هر که از مادر زاد

١٩١

کم کن طمعِ جهان که باشی خرسند

از نیک و بدِ زمانه بگسل پیوند

خوشباش چنانکه هست این دورِ فلک

هم بگذرد و نماند این دوری چند

hand of each." "Beyond his nature," *i.e.* beyond the limits of his own thought.

191. C. L. N. A. B. I. The readings vary considerably. *Hast i daur*, etc., The existence of the wheel of heaven.

h

192.

What eye can pierce the veil of God's decree,
Or read the riddle of earth's destinies?
    Pondered have I for years three-score and
        twelve,
    And can but say these things are mysteries.

193.

They say, when the last trump shall sound its
        knell,
Our Friend will sternly judge, and doom to hell.
    Can aught but good from perfect goodness
        come?
Compose your trembling hearts, 't will all be
        well.

194.

Drink wine to clear away vain scruples' weeds,
And tangle of the two-and-seventy creeds:
    Do not forswear that wondrous alchemy,
    'T will turn to gold, and cure a thousand needs

---

192. C. L. N. A. I.   So Job "The thunder of his power
who can understand?"
    193   C. L. N. A. I. J. H.   Juzi, (?) juz a-
    194. C. L. N. A. B. I   Muhammad said, "My people

۱۹۲

کس را پسِ پردهٔ قضا راه نشد
وز سرِّ قدر هیچ کس آگاه نشد
هفتاد و دو سال فکر کردم شب و روز
معلوم نگشت و قصّه کوتاه نشد

۱۹۳

گویند بحشر گفتگو خواهد بود
وان یارِ عزیز تندخو خواهد بود
از خیرِ محض جز نکوئی ناید
خوشباش که عاقبت نکو خواهد بود

۱۹۴

می خور که ز دل کثرت و قلّت ببرد
و اندیشهٔ هفتاد و دو ملّت ببرد
پرهیز مکن ز کیمیائی که ازو
یکمن بخوری هزار علّت ببرد

---

shall be divided into seventy-three sects, all of which, save one, shall have their portion in the fire." Pocock, Specimen 210. *Kasrat wa qillat*, excess and defect; scruples as to the true via media.

195.

'Tis true, wine is forbidden, but this ban
Regards the place, the quantum, and the man :
  When all these three are fitting, prithee say,
Cannot a wise man drink ?   If not, who can ?

196.

To fill a gallon beaker I design,
And prime myself with two great cups of
      wine ;
  Old faith and reason thrice will I divorce,
Then take to wife the daughter of the vine.

197.

True, I drink wine, like every man of sense,
For I know Allah will not take offence .
  Before time was, He knew that I should drink,
And who am I to flout his prescience ?

---

195   C. L N. A. B. I.   A hit at the casuistry on the
subject of wine.
  196.   C. N. A. I.   A triple divorce is irrevocable   Koran,
ii 230.

۱۹۵

می گرچه حرامست ولی تا که خورد

و آنگاه چه، مقدار و دگر با که خورد

هرگاه که این سه شرط شد راست بگو

گر می نخورد مردمِ دانا که خورد

۱۹۶

من باده بجامِ یکمنی خواهم کرد

خودرا بدو جامِ می غنی خواهم کرد

اوّل سه طلاقِ عقل و دین خواهم داد

پس دخترِ رز را بزنی خواهم کرد

۱۹۷

من می خورم و هر که چو من اهل بود

می خوردنِ او نزدِ خدا سهل بود

می خوردنِ من حقّ از ازل میدانست

گر من نخورم علمِ خدا جهل بود

---

197   C L N A. B I H.   Ascribed in the Táríkh i
Quzída to Siráj ud Din Qumrí.   (Jonrn. R.A S., xxxii.
p. 756

198.

Wine-bibbers fall from wealth to misery,
And by their rioting the world defy;
   Place in my ruby pipe some emerald hemp.
'Twill serve as well to blind care's serpent eye.

199.

These dullards never burn the midnight oil
In deep research, nor do they ever toil
   To step beyond themselves, but dress them
      fine,
And others' reputation try to spoil.

200.

What time false dawn displays its cold grey
      light,
Handle thy cup of wine well racked and bright,
   Truth, it is said, tastes bitter in the mouth.
This is a proof that wine is truth and right

---

198   C L N. A I   Scan af ânî.   The emerald is supposed to have the virtue of blinding serpents

199.   C. L. N A. I.   Shâmé chand   Vullers (p. 253)

۱۹۸

میخواره اگر غنی بود عُور شود
وز عُربده اش جهان پر از شُور شود
در حقّهء لعل زان زمرّد ریزم
تا دیدهء افعیِ غمم کُور شود

۱۹۹

نابُرده بصبح در طلب شامی چند
ننهاده ز خویشتن برون گامی چند
در کسوتِ خاص آمده عامی چند
بدنام کنندهء نکونامی چند

۲۰۰

وقتی که طلوعِ صبحِ ازرق باشد
باید بکفت جامِ مروّقی باشد
گویند که حق تلخ بود در افواه
باید که بدین دلیل می حق باشد

<hr>

takes this *ya* to be *yá i tankír*; and Lumsden (ıı 269) as
the *yá i tansífí*

200. C. L N. A. I. J. False dawn, the faint light
before sunrise.

201.

Now is the time earth decks her verdant bowers,

And trees, like Musa's hand, grow white with
    flowers !

  As 't were by 'Isa's breath the plants revive,

While clouds brim o'er, like tearful eyes, with
    showers.

202.

O burden not thyself with drudgery,

Lord of white silver and red gold to be ;

  But feast with friends, ere this warm breath
    of thine

Be chilled in death, and earthworms feast on
    thee.

203.

The showers of grape-juice, which cupbearers
    pour,

Quench fires of grief in many a sad heart's core.

  Give praise to Allah, and deem wine a balm

To purge your griefs and heal affliction sore !

---

201 C. L N A. B I. *Musa* and *'Isa* are often written
without the *alif i maqsúra* Bl., Prosody, 3.

202 N *Tá i tajalul.* "See you do not "

٢٠١

وقتست که از سبزه جهان آرایند

موسیٰ صفتان ز شاخ کف بنُمایند

عیسیٰ صفتان ز خاک بیرون آیند

وز چشمِ سحاب چشمها بکُشایند

٢٠٢

هان تا ننهی برتنِ خود غصّه و درد

تا جمع کنی سیمِ سفید و زرِ زرد

زان پیش که گردد نفسِ گرمِ تو سرد

با دوست بخور که دشمنت خواهد خورْد

٢٠٣

هر جُرعه که ساقیش بجام افشاند

در دیدهٔ گرم آتشِ غم بنُشاند

سبحان اللّٰه ز باده میپنداری

آبی که ز صد درد دلت بُرهاند

---

203. C. L. N. A. B. I. In line 1 some MSS. read *bakhák*. *Dídayi garm*, 'eyes of anguish.' Scan *garm átíshí* (*Alif i wasl*).

201.

Can alien zealots all Thy kindness tell,
Like us who in Thy intimacy dwell?
    Thou say'st, "All sinners will I burn with
      fire."
Say that to strangers, *we* know Thee too well.

205.

O comrades dear, when hither ye repair
In times to come, communion sweet to share.
    While the cupbearer pours you old Magh wine,
Call poor Khayyám to mind, and breathe a
    prayer.

206.

For me heaven's sphere no music ever made,
Nor yet with soothing voice my fears allayed:
    If e'er I gained a breathing-space of joy,
Into woe's grip I was at once betrayed.

---

204 N *Bakaram*, query *karam i*.
205 L. N. B. *Mâyî*. The second *ya* is the *yá i batni*

٢٠٤

زاهد بتكرم ترا چو ما نشْناسد

بيگانه، ترا چو آشنا نشْناسد

گفتی كه گنه كنی بدوزخ برمت

اینرا بتكسی گو كه ترا نشْناسد

٢٠٥

یاران چو باتّفاقی میعاد كنید

خودرا بجمال یكدگر شاد كنید

ساقی چو مئی مغانه بر كف گیرد

بیچاره فلانرا بدعا یاد كنید

٢٠٦

یكروز فلك كار مرا ساز ند(اد

هرگز سوی من دمی خوش آواز ندّاد

یكروز دمی ز شادمانی نزدم

كانروز بدستِ صد غمم باز ندّاد

before the attribute *Mughána*. *Fulán ra*, "poor such an one."
206. C. L. N. A. I.

207.

Sooner with half a loaf contented be,
And water from a broken crock, like me,
        Than lord it over your inferiors,
Or to your equals bow the vassal knee.

208.

While Moon and Venus in the sky shall dwell,
None shall see aught red grape-juice to excel:
        O foolish publicans, what can you buy
One half so precious as the goods you sell?

209.

They who, renowned for lore and power of brain,
As "Guiding Lights" men's homage did obtain,
        Not even they emerged from this dark night,
But told their dreams, and fell asleep again!

---

207   C. L. N. A I. In line 2, note *izáfat* dropped after
silent *he. Kam az khud*, "one less than yourself." Vullers,
p. 254

٢٠٧

یکسان بدو روز اگر شود حاصلِ مرد

وز کوزهٔ شکستهٔ دمِ آبی سرد

مخدومِ کم از خودی چرا باید بود

یا خدمتِ چون خودی چرا باید کرد

٢٠٨

تا زهره و مه در آسمان گشت پدید

بهتر ز مئی لعل کسی هیچ ندید

من در عجبم ز میفروشان کایشان

به زانچه فروشند چه خواهند خرید

٢٠٩

آنانکه محیطِ فضل و آداب شدند

از جمعِ کملِ شمعِ اصحاب شدند

ره زین شبِ تاریک نبردند برون

گفتند فسانهٔ و در خواب شدند

---

208. C. L. N. A. B. I. B.'s first two lines differ. Ethé
compares this with some lines by Kisāi: Lieder des Kisai,
p. 145.

209. C. L. N. A. I. J. *Fisánayé yá i tankír.*

210.

At dawn, when dews bedeck the tulip's face,
And violets their heavy heads abase,

I love to see the roses' folded buds,
With petals closed against the winds' disgrace.

211.

Like as the skies rain down sweet jessamine,
And sprinkle all the meads with eglantine,

So, in the fashion of those violet skies,
I pour in lily cups my rosy wine.

212.

Ah! thou hast snared this head, though white
       as snow,
Which oft has vowed the wine-cup to forego:

And wrecked the mansion long resolve did
       build,
And rent the vesture penitence did sew!

---

210. L B.

211 B Here read *mäyi*, with one *yi*, and *hasia*,
because the metre requires a word of only two consonants,
and two short vowels, of the *uazn māīā*.

٢١٠

هر صبح که روی لاله شبنم گیرد

بالای بنفشه در چمن خم گیرد

انصاف مرا ز غنچه خوش می آید

کو دامن خویشتن فراهم گیرد

٢١١

گردون ز سحاب نسترن می ریزد

گوئی که شگوفه در چمن می ریزد

در جام چو سوسن می گلگون ریزم

کز ابر بنفشه گون سمن می ریزد

٢١٢

پیرانه سرم عشق تو در دام کشید

ورنه ز کجا دست من و جام نبید

آن توبه که عقل داد جانان بشکست

وان جامه که صبر دوخت ایّام درید

---

212. B. *Nabíd* is often written *nabíz*, probably a survival from the time when *dals* were dotted. Bl., Prosody, 17.

213.

I am not one whom Death doth much dismay,
Life's terrors all Death's terrors far outweigh;
   This life, that Heaven hath lent me for a
      while,
I will pay back, when it is time to pay.

214.

The stars, who dwell on heaven's exalted stage,
Mock the prognosticators of our age:
   Take heed, hold fast the rope of mother wit,
These augurs all mistrust their own presage.

215.

The people who the heavenly world adorn.
Who come each night, and go away each morn.
   Now on heaven's skirt, and now in earth's
      deep pouch,
While Allah lives, will aye anew be born!

---

213. C. L. A. B I   B reads *nim* for *him* in line 2.

214 L B. A hit at the astrologers.

۲۱۳

آن مرد نِیَم کز عدمم بیم آید
آن بیم مرا خوشتر ازین بیم آید
جانیست مرا بعاریة داده خدا
تسلیم کنم چو وقتِ تسلیم آید

۲۱۴

اجرام که ساکنانِ این ایوانند
اسبابِ تردّدِ خردمندانند
هان تا سرِ رشتهٔ خرد گم نکنی
کانان که مدبّرند سرگردانند

۲۱۵

آنها که فلک ریزهٔ دهْر آرایند
آیند و روند و باز با دهْر آیند
در دامنِ آسمان و در جیبِ زمین
خلقیست که تا خدا نمیرد زایند

---

215. L. B. Earth's pouch, *i.e.* "beneath the earth."
Falak rēzǎǐ, L. reads *falak dǐdǎǐ* and the Dabistān i
Muzāhib (Calcutta edition, p. 187) quotes it as *falak zahrǎǐ*.

216.

The slaves of intellect and theory,

Worn out with " Being " and " Nonentity,"

Get shrivelled up like old dried grapes,—the
fools—

Go, drink grape-juice, and ignoramus be !

217.

Sense, seeking happiness, bids us pursue

Sweets of this life that lasts a breath or two ;

She says, we are not as the garden herb,

Which, when they cut it down, springs up
anew.

218.

Now Ramazán is past, Shawwál comes back,

And mirth and quips and cranks no more we
lack ;

Now droves of wine-skin carriers throng the
street,

Crying " Ho ! here's the porter with his pack "

_ - -

216   B. L   *Tamyíz*, "power of drawing distinctions."
Freytag   *Míríz*, archaic for *mureíz*. In line 3, L reads
bákhabarán.

۲۱۶

آنها که اسیرِ عقل و تمییز شدند

در حسرتِ هست و نیست ناچیز شدند

رو بیخبری و آبِ انگور گزین

کاین بیخبران بغوره میویز شدند

۲۱۷

آن عقل که در راهِ سعادت پوئید

روزی صد بار خود ترا می گوئید

دریاب تو این یکدمه وقتت که نهٔ

آن ترّه که بدُروند و دیگر روئید

۲۱۸

ماهِ رمضان برفت و شوّال آمد

هنگامِ نشاط و عیش و قوّال آمد

آمد گه آنکه خیکها اندر دوش

گویند که پشت پشت حمّال آمد

---

217. C. L. A. B. I. J. *Goyid*, from *goyidan.* Cp.
Moschus on the Mallows (Idyll, iii. 106).

218. B. *Pusht pusht*, "one after another," like *pusht
ba pusht*, "generation after generation."

219.

My comrades all are gone ; Death, deadly foe,
Hath caught them one by one, and trampled
    low ;
   They shared life's feast, and drank its wine
    with me,
But lost their heads, and dropped a while ago.

220.

They whose repute by every mouth is spread,
Who stand in streets to beg a crust of bread,
   Say, " We are Shiblis and Junaids." I grant
That in aridity they're born and bred!

221.

When the great Founder moulded me of old,
He mixed much baser metal with my gold ;
   Better or fairer I can never be
Than what I was when fresh from Allah's mould.

---

219   C. L A. I   Quoted by *Badáúní*, ii. 159.
220   C L A. I.   L reads *bahahna namad*, but the line
will not scan with that reading. Shibli, Junaid, and Ma'ruf
i Kharkh, " the hero of Karkh" (a suburb of Baghdad) were

۲۱۹

یاران موافق همه از دست شدند

در پای اجل یگان یگان پست شدند

بودند بیك شراب در مجلس عمْر

دَوری دو سه پیشتر ز ما مست شدند

۲۲۰

آنان كه بمكهنه و بنو موصوفند

در ره بكف آب و دو نان موقوفند

گویند كه شبلی و جنیدیم همه

شبلی نه ولی در کرخی معروفند

۲۲۱

تا خاك مرا بقالب آمیخته اند

بس فتنه كه از خاك بر انگیخته اند

من بهتر ازین نمی توانم بودن

کز بوته مرا چنین برون ریخته اند

---

saints. The pun on Karkh and *Kārākhī*, "aridity" is untranslatable.

221. C. L. A. I.

222.

The joyous souls who quaff potations deep,
And saints who in the mosque sad vigils keep,
 Are lost at sea alike, and find no shore,
ONE only wakes, all others are asleep.

223.

Notbeing's water served to mix my clay,
And on my heart the fires of sorrow prey,
 And blown am I like wind about the world,
And last my crumbling earth is swept away.

224.

Small gains to learning on this earth accrue.
They pluck life's fruitage, learning who eschew;
 Take pattern by the fools who learning shun,
And then perchance shall fortune smile on you.

---

222. L. B   One, *i e.* the Deity
223. L.   This introduction of the four elements in one quatrain is called *Mutazádd*   Gladwin, p 60

٢٢٢

آنها که کشندهٔ نبیذِ ناب اند

و انها که بشب مدام در محراب اند

بر خشک یکی نیست همه در آب اند

بیدار یکیست دیگران در خواب اند

٢٢٣

از آبِ عدم تخم مرا کاشته اند

از آتشِ غم روحِ من افراشته اند

سرگشته چو باد دمبدم گردِ جهان

تا خاکِ من ز جای بر داشته اند

٢٢٤

چون نیست درین زمانه سودی ز خرد

جز بیخرد از زمانه بر می خورد

پیش آور زانکه او خرد را ببرد

تا بو که زمانه سویِ ما بر نگرد

---

224 C L A I. *Bú* contracted from *buwad*, as *bŭd*
from búd Bibarad, " throws away "

225.

When the fair Spirit doth this house vacate,
Each element resumes its primal state,
  And these four strands of life, like threads of
    silk,
Are all unravelled by the blows of fate.

226.

These people string their beads of learned
    lumber,
And tell of Allah stories without number;
  But never solve the riddle of the skies,
So wag the chin, and get them back to slumber.

227.

These folk are half-starved asses of the street,
Skins full of empty air, like drums to beat;
  They're humble slaves of all who have a
    name;
Get you a name, and they will kiss your feet.

---

225. C. L A I *Abrésham tab'*, like *Hátim tab'*.
226. L. Possibly a hit at the *Mutakallamín*, or
scholastic theologians.

٢٢٥

چون شاهدِ روحِ خانه پرداز شود

هر جنس باصلِ خویشتن باز شود

این سازِ وجودِ چار ابریشم طبع

از زخمهٔء روزگار بیساز شود

٢٢٦

انها که بفکر درِّ معنی سفتند

در ذاتِ خداوند سخنها گفتند

واقف چو نگشتند بر اسرارِ فلك

اوّل زبخی زدند و آخر خفتند

٢٢٧

این خلق همه خرانِ با افسوس اند

پر مشعله و میان تهی چون کوس اند

خواهی که کفِ پای ترا می بوسند

خوش نام بزی که بندهٔء ناموس اند

---

227. C. L. A. I. *Bá afsós* is an epithet, like *bá khabar*,
and hence *kharán*, the noun qualified by it, takes the *izáfat*.
Lumsden, ii. 259. *Pur mush'ila*, &c., "the leather case
full, but the inside empty," *i.e.* windbags.

228.

On the dread day of final scrutiny,
As is thy wisdom so thy meed shall be;
  Strive to get virtues here, for thou wilt rise
Bearing the imprint of thy quality.

229.

Great store of heads, like bowls, the Brazier
    made,
And His own likeness in each one portrayed;
  One He inverted o'er the board of life,
Whereat we men are evermore dismayed.

230.

My true condition I may thus explain
In two short verses, which the whole contain :
  " From love to Thee I now lay down my life,
In hope Thy Love will raise me up again."

---

228. C. L A I.
229 C. L A. I   " One inverted," i e the sky. Kánsa
is also spelled kása.

٢٢٨

روزی که جزایِ هر صفت خواهد بود
قدْرِ تو بقدْرِ معرفت خواهد بود
در حسنِ صفت کوش که در روزِ جزا
حشرِ تو بصورتِ صفت خواهد بود

٢٢٩

آن کاسه گری که کاسهٔء سرها کرد
در کاسه گری صفاتِ خود پیدا کرد
بر خوانِ وجودِ ما نگون کاسه نهاد
وان کاسهٔء سرِ نگون پر از سودا کرد

٢٣٠

از واقعهٔء ترا خبر خواهم کرد
وان را بدو حرف مختصر خواهم کرد
با عشقِ تو در خاك فرو خواهم شد
با مهرِ تو سر ز خاك بر خواهم کرد

---

230 C. L. A I Scan *wáḱ'áyi* Here *hamza* plus
kasra stands for *ya i tankh* "The actual s'ate of the
case "

231.

The heart's a lamp kindled at beauty's eyes,
And gaining life from that whereby it dies;
    Like lamp with moth, 'tis occupied with
       those
Who make themselves a burning sacrifice.

232.

For him that's good my very life I'd sell,
Yea, though he trod me down, I'd count it
      well;
    Men say, "Inform us what and where is
      hell?"
Bad company will make this earth a hell.

233.

The sun doth smite the roofs with Orient ray,
And, Khosrau-like, his wine-red sheen display;
    Arise, and drink! the herald of the dawn
Proclaims the advent of another day.

---

231 L Metre Ramal, No 50 In line 3 the first
syllable is short See Bl. Prosody, p. 43 In this form
the metre is like Horace's "*Miseraium est*," etc. Odes,
iii. 12

٢٣١

دل چراغیست که نور از رخِ دلبر گیرد

ور بمیرد ز غمش زندگی از سر گیرد

صفتِ شمع به پروانه دلی باید گفت

کین حدیثست که با سوختگان در گیرد

٢٣٢

جانم بفدایِ آنکه او اهْل بود

سر در قدمش اگر نهم سهْل بود

خواهی که بدانی بیقین دوزخ را

دوزخ بجهان صحبتِ نا اهل بود

٢٣٣

خورشید کمندِ صبح بر بام افگنْد

کی خسرَوِ روز باده در جام افگند

می خور که منادیِ سحرگه خیزان

آوازه ز سرِ نو در ایّام افگند

---

232. C. L. A. I. Also ascribed to Hafiz. (Brockhaus, No. 668.)

233. C. L. A. I. J. Readings vary. I follow L. in *zi sar i nu*, adding a *tashdid ob metrum*.

234.

Comrades ! whene'er ye meet together here,
Recall to mind the friend ye once held dear ;
    And, when the wine-cups reach his vacant
        seat,
Spill a few drops his thirsty dust to cheer.

235.

Why didst Thou at the first pour down on me
Such favours and such sweet prosperity,
    And now endeavour to afflict my heart?
What is it I have done to anger Thee ?

236.

The men who to mere form such deference show
Divorce that body from its soul, I trow ;
    If, like a beaker, they will don a comb,
My beaker here of wine I will forego !

---

234.   B   A variation of No 205.

235.   B   So Job, " He multipheth my wounds without
cause "

٢٣٤

یاران بموافقت چو میعاد کنید

باید که ز دوست یادِ بسیار کند

چون بادهٔ خوشگوار نوشید بهم

نوبت چو بما رسد نـگونسار کنید

٢٣٥

چندان کرم و لطف ز آغاز چه بود

وان داشتنم در طرب و ناز چه بود

اکنون همه در رنجِ دلم میکوشی

آخر چه گناه کرده ام باز چه بود

٢٣٦

انها که اساسِ کار بر زرق نهند

آیند و میانِ جان و تن فرق نهند

بر فرقِ نهمِ خروسِ می را پس ازین

گر همچو خروسم ارّه بر فرق نهند

---

236. L. B. "*Arra*, a saw, a cock's comb." See Pandnama, p. 2 (Ouseley, Oriental Collections, II. 127). "If they will put on their heads a saw" (comb), *i.e.* saw off their head. *Bar faraq* in line 3. "put aside."

237.

Many have come, and run their eager race,
Striving for riches, luxuries, or place,
    And quaffed their wine, and now all silent lie,
Enfolded in their parent earth's embrace.

238.

Then, when the good receive their portions due,
To this poor wretch will fall a portion too;
    If good, I shall be numbered *with* the good,
If wicked, *through* the good find mercy too !

239.

Of happy turns of fortune take your fill,
Seek pleasure's couch and wine-cup, if you will;
    Allah regards not if you sin, or saint it,
So take your pleasure, be it good or ill.

---

237. C. L A. I
238. C. L. A I.   So in the Bostan, *Badānrā ba nēkān
hi bakshand,* "They will pardon the bad for the sake of the
good"

٢٣٧

آنها كه در آمدند در جوش شدند

آشفتهٴ ناز و طرب و نوش شدند

خوردند پيالهٴ و خاموش شدند

در خاكِ ابد جمله هم آغوش شدند

٢٣٨

فردا كه نصيبِ نيك بختان بخشند

قسمى بمنِ رندِ پريشان بخشند

گر نيك آيم مرا از ايشان شمرند

ور بد باشم مرا بد يشان بخشند

٢٣٩

از گردشِ روزگار بهرى بر گير

بر تختِ طرب نشين بكف ساغر گير

از طاعت و معصيت خدا مستغنيست

بارى تو مرادِ خود ز عالم بر گير

---

239 C L N. A. I J Alluding to the *Hadis* " These
are in heaven, and Allah regards not their sins, and these
in hell, and Allah regards not their good works" See
Gulshan i Ráz, p 55.

M

240.

Heaven multiplies our sorrows day by day,

And grants no joys it does not take away;

    If those unborn could know the ills we bear,

What think you, would they rather come or
       stay?

241.

Why ponder thus the future to foresee,

And wear thyself with vain anxiety?

    Cast off thy care, leave Allah's plans to Him,

He formed them all without consulting thee.

242.

The tenants of the tombs to dust decay,

Nescient of self and all beside are they;

    Their sundered atoms float about the world,

Like mirage clouds, until the judgment-day.

---

240. C. L N. A I. J. This recalls Byron's " Stanzas
for Music"

241. C. L N A. I. J.

٢٤٠

افلاك كه جز غم نفزایند دگر

ننهند بجا تا نربایند دگر

نا آمدگان اگر بدانند كه ما

از دهر چه میکشیم نایند دگر

٢٤١

از بودنی ای دوست چه داری تیمار

وز فکرتِ بیهوده دل و جان افگار

خرّم تو بزی جهان بشادی گذران

تدبیر نه با تو کرده اند اوّل کار

٢٤٢

این اهلِ قبور خاك گشتند و غبار

بیخود شده و بیخبرند از همه كار

هر ذرّه ز هر ذرّه گرفتند کنار

آه این چه سرابست كه تا روزِ شمار

<hr>

242. C. L. N. A. I. J. Line 4, " What a mirage is
this, which (lasts) till the judgment day." Some MSS.
read *sharab*, and alter the order of the lines.

243.

O soul ! lay up all earthly goods in store,
Thy mead with pleasure's flowerets spangle o'er:
    And know 'tis all as dew, that decks the
        flowers
For one short night, and then is seen no more !

244.

Heed not traditions, forms, or discipline ;
So that you injure none and none malign,
    And ne'er withhold your store from worthy
        men,
I guarantee you heaven—and now some wine !

245.

Vexed by this wheel of things, that pets the base,
My sorrow-laden life wears on apace ;
    Like rosebud, from the storm I wrap me close.
Like tulip, blood-spots on my bosom trace.

---

243. C. L. N A I J   There are several variations of
this.
    244. C. L N A B I. J.   See Koran, ii 172 . " There
is no piety in turning your faces to the east or west, but he

٢٤٣

ای دل همه اسباب جهان خواسته گیر
باغِ طربت بسبزه آراسته گیر
وانگاه بران سبزه شبی چون شبنم
بنشسته و بامداد بر خاسته گیر

٢٤٤

سنّت مکن و فریضهارا بگذار
وان لقمه که داری ز کسان باز مدار
غیبت مکن و مجوی کسرا آزار
هم وعدهٔ آن جهان مذم باده بیار

٢٤٥

از گردشِ این زمانهٔ دون پرور
با صد غم و درد میبرم عمر بسر
چون غنچه بگلزارِ جهان با دل تنگی
چون لاله ز باغِ دهر با خونِ جگر

---

is pious who believeth in God . . . . and disburseth his
wealth to the needy," etc.

245. N.

246.

Now 'tis the time of youth, the time for wine,
For boon companions, and for generous wine!
  As this vain world was wasted by the flood,
Go you and lay you waste with floods of wine!

247.

The world is baffled in its search for Thee!
Wealth cannot find Thee, no, nor poverty;
  All speak of Thee, but none have ears to hear,
Thou 'rt near to all, but none have eyes to see.

248.

Take care you never hold a drinking bout
With an ill-tempered, ill-conditioned lout;
  He'll make a vile disturbance all night long,
And vile apologies next day, no doubt.

---

246 C N A. I. J.

247. N So Hafiz, Ode 355 (Brockhaus):
    "How can our eyes behold Thee as Thou art?"

۲۴۶

ایّام جوانیست شراب اولیتر

با خوش پسران بادهٔ ناب اولیتر

این عالم ِ فانی چو خرابست باب

از باده در او مست و خراب اولیتر

۲۴۷

ای در طلب ِ تو عالمی در شر و شور

در پیش ِ تو درویش و توانگر همه عور

ای با همه در حدیث و گوش ِ همه کر

وی با همه در حضور و چشم ِ همه کور

۲۴۸

با سفلهٔ تند خوی و بیعقل و وقار

زینهار مخور باده که رنج آرد بار

بدمستی و شور و عربده درشب عیش

درد ِ سر و عذر خواهیش روز ِ خمار

'Álamé. "a world," or 'Álamí, "a denizen of the world."

248. C. L. N. A. I. J. In line 3 scan *badmastīyŏ*, and in line 4 *Khwáhīyásh*.

249.

Not always are the inconstant stars benign ;
Why toil then after vain desires, and pine
 To lade thyself with load of fortune's boons?
Drop it thou must—and drop this life of thine.

250.

O comrades ! here is filtered wine, come drink !
Pledge all your charming sweethearts, as you
  drink ;
 'Tis the grape's blood, and this is what it
  says,
" To you I dedicate my life-blood ! drink ! "

251.

Are you depressed ? then take of *bang* one grain,
Of rosy grape-juice take one pint or twain ;
 Sufis, you say, must not take this or that,
Then go and eat the pebbles off the plain !

---

249 C L N A I J

250 C L N A I. J *Halál karda am,* " I have made
lawful by shedding it."

251 N. In lines 1 and 2 scan *yakjáwáki* and *mănáki,*

٢٤٩

چون نیست ز اختر آنکه رو داد قرار
چندین ز پی‌ئی مرادِ دل رنج مدار
هان تا ننهی بر دلِ خود چندین بار
بگذاشتن و گذشتن است اخر کار

٢٥٠.

جانا می صافِ نا مشوّش میخور
بر یادِ بتانِ نغزِ دلکش می خور
می خونِ رز است و رز ترا میگوید
خون بر تو حلال کرده ام خوش می خور

٢٥١

دلتنگ شوی یکجوکی بنگ بخور
یا یک منگی بادهٔ گلرنگ بخور
صوفی شدهٔ این نخوری آن نخوری
در خورِد تو سنگست برو سنگ بخور

ak being the diminutive, and *yá* the *yá i taukír*, displacing the *izáfat*: Lumsden, ii. 269. *Bang*, a narcotic, made of hemp. *Dar khward i tu*, "fit for you."

252.

I saw a busy potter by the way
Kneading with might and main a lump of clay;
   And, lo! the clay cried, "Use me tenderly,
I was a man myself but yesterday!"

253.

Oh! wine is richer than the realm of Jam,
More fragrant than the food of Miriam;
   Sweeter are sighs that topers heave at morn
Than strains of Bu Sa'íd and Bin Adham.

254.

Deep in the rondure of the heavenly blue,
There is a cup, concealed from mortal view,
   Which all must drink in turn; O sigh not
      then,
But drink it gladly, when it comes to you!

252 C. L N A B. I. J _Hál_, ecstasy

253. C. L N. A l. J For the quatrains of Abú Sa'íd
bin Abi'l Khair (d 440 A H), see Ethe and S Those
ascribed to Ibráhím bin Adham (d 106 A H) are apo-

٢٥٢

دی کوزه‌گری بدیدم اندر بازار

بر تازه گلی لگد همی زد بسیار

وان گل بزبانِ حال با وی میگفت

من همچو تو بوده ام مرا نیکو دار

٢٥٣

یکجرعه مَی از مملکتِ جم خوشتر

بویِ قدح از غذایِ مریم خوشتر

آه سحری ز سینهٔ خمّاری

از نالهٔ بو سعید و ادهم خوشتر

٢٥٤

در دائرهٔ سپهر ناپیدا غَور

جامیست که جمله را چشانید بدَور

نوبت چو بدورِ تو رسد آه مکن

می نوش بخوشدلی که دورست بجَور

---

cryphal, "Miriam's food," see Koran, xix. 24.

254. C. L. A. I. J. *Daur ast ba jaur*, "it is the time
for a bumper."

255.

Though you should live to four or forty score,

Go hence you must, as all have gone before ;

　　Then, be you king, or beggar of the streets,

They 'll rate you all the same, no less, no more.

256.

If you seek Him, abandon child and wife,

Forsake, and sever all these ties to life :

　　All these are bonds that check your upward
　　　　course.

Arise, and cut these bonds, as with a knife.

257.

O heart ! this world is but a hollow show,

Why should its empty griefs distress thee so ?

　　Bow down, and bear thy fate, the eternal pen

Will not unwrite its roll for thee, I trow !

---

255. L

256   L. B   So *Gulshan i Ráz*, 1 911   Comp St
Luke, xiv 26

۲۵۵

عمرِ تو چه دو صد و چه سیصد چه هزار

زین کهنه سرا برون برندت ناچار

گر بادشهی و گـر گدای بازار

این هر دو بیك نرخ بُوَد آخر کار

۲۵۶

اورا خواهـی ز زن و فرزند ببُر

مردانه در آز خویش و پیوند ببُر

هر چیز که هست بندِ راهست ترا

با بند چگونه ره روی بند ببُر

۲۵۷

ای دل چو حقیقت جهانست مجاز

چندین چه خوری تو غم ازین رنجِ دراز

تن را بقضا سپار و با درد بساز

کین رفته قلم ز بهرِ تو ناید باز

---

257. L. N. B. The "pen" is that with which Allah
writes his decrees. Koran, lxviii. 1.

258.

Who e'er returned of all that went before,
To tell of that long road they travel o'er ?

Leave naught undone of what you have to do,
For when you go, you will return no more.

259.

This wheel that doth to none its aims explain
Full many a Mahmud and Ayaz hath slain ;

Come, let us drink, they grant us not two lives,
When one is spent, we find it not again.

260.

Prophet, o'er kings predominant in might,
Know'st thou when wine can make our spirits
        light ?

On Sunday, Monday, Tuesday, Wednesday,
        Thursday,
Friday, and Saturday, both day and night !

---

258. C. N L A I J. *Imādāyē, yá i tankir.*

259 L N Mahmud, the celebrated king of Ghazna,
and Ayáz his favourite. Scan *wáyáz (aly i wasl).*

٢٥٨

از جملهٔ رفتگانِ این راهِ دراز
باز آمدهٔ کو که بما گوید راز
زبنهار درین سراچه از روی مجا
چیزی نگذاری که نمیآئی باز

٢٥٩

این چرخ که با کسی نمیگوید راز
کشته بسِتم هـزار محمود و ایاز
میخور که بکس عمر دو باره ندهد
هرکس که شد از جهان نمیآید باز

٢٦٠

ای بر همه سرورانِ عالم فیروز
دانی که چه وقت می بود روح افروز
یکشنبه و دو شنبه و سه شنبه و چار
پنجشنبه و آدینه و شنبه شب و روز

---

260 C. L. N. A. I. J. The *jim in panjshamba* is dropped in scanning See Bl, Prosody, p 10. In line 4 note silent *he* in *shamba* scanned long as well as short.

261.

O turn away those roguish eyes of thine !
Be still ! seek not my peace to undermine !
 Thou say'st, " Look not." I might as well
  essay
To tip my goblet, and not spill my wine.

262.

In taverns better far commune with Thee,
Than pray in mosques and fail Thy face to see !
 O first and last of all Thy creatures Thou :
'Tis Thine to burn and Thine to cherish me !

263.

To wise and worthy men your time devote.
But from the worthless keep your walk remote :
 Dare to take poison from a sage's hand,
But from a fool refuse an antidote.

261　N　Line 1, a proverb denoting an impossibility.
262.　C. L N A B I J　This is clearly an address

٢٦١

ای خوش پسرِ غمزهگرِ رنگ آمیز

بنشین و هزار فتنه بنشان و مخیز

تو حکم همیکنی که در من منگر

این حکم چنان بود که کج دار و مریز

٢٦٢

با تو بخرابات اگر گویم راز

به زانکه کنم بیتو بمحراب نماز

ای اوّل و آخرِ همه خلقان تو

خواهی تو مرا بسوز و خواهی بنواز

٢٦٣

با مردمِ پاکباز و عاقل آمیز

از نا اهلان هزار فرسنگ گریز

گر زهر دهد ترا خردمند بنوش

ور نوش دهد ز دست نا اهل بریز

---

to the Deity, so tavern must be understood mystically. See
Gulshan i Ráz, l. 839.

263. L. N. Line 2 is in metre 17.

264.

I flew here, like a bird from the wild, in aim
Up to a higher nest my course to frame:

But, finding here no guide who knows the way,
Fly out by the same door where through I
    came.

265.

He made the law we strive against in vain,
Then bade us from observing it refrain;

'Twixt law and counterlaw we're in a strait.
" Tip up your jar, but all your wine retain."

266.

They pass away, and none is seen returning,
To teach that other world's recondite learning:

'Twill not be shown for dull mechanic prayers,
For prayer is naught without true heartfelt
    yearning.

---

264   C L. N A I J   See Green Short History p 20,
for a similar parable   Bu for buried.
265   L N   Hukmi', the natural " law in the members
as opposed to the divine law   Cp. Quatrain 434, and Lord

۲٦٤

بازی بودم پریده از عالمِ راز

تا بو که رسم من از نشیبی بفراز

اینجا چو نیافتم کسی محرمِ راز

زان درکه در آمدم برون رفتم باز

۲٦٥

حکمی که از او محال باشد پرهیز

فرموده و امر کرده کزوی بگریز

آنگاه میان امر و نهیش عاجز

درمانده جهانیان که کج دار و مریز

۲٦٦

رفتند و ز رفتگان یکی نامد باز

تا با تو بگوید سخن از پردهٔ راز

کارت ز نیاز میکشاید نه نماز

بازیچه بُوَد نماز بی صِدْق و نیاز

Brooke in Ward's English Poets, I. 370.

266. C. L. N. A. I. The *formal* prayers of Moslems are
rather ascriptions of praise, and repetitions of texts, than
petitions.

267.

Go to ! Cast dust on those deaf skies, who spurn
Thy orisons and bootless prayers, and learn
    To quaff the cup, and hover round the
        fair ;
Of all who go, did ever one return ?

268.

No pearls of righteousness do I enlace,
Nor sweep the dust of sin from off my face,
    Yet since I never counted One as two,
I do not quite despair of heavenly grace.

269.

Again to tavern haunts do we repair,
And bid "Adieu" to the five hours of prayer :
    Where'er we see a long-necked flask of
        wine,
Our necks we elongate that wine to share.

---

267. C. L. N. A. B 1 J. An answer to the last
  268 C L. N A. B I J. *Tauhid,* or Unitarianism, is
the central doctrine of Islám So Hafiz, Ode 465. The
poet hopes to be saved for his faith, if not for his works.

٢٦٧

رو بر سرِ افلاك جهانِ خاك انداز

می میخور و گردِ خوبرویان میتاز

چه جایِ عبادتست و چه جایِ نماز

کز جمله روندگان یکی نامد باز

٢٦٨

گر گوهرِ طاعتت نسفتم هرگز

گردِ گنه از چهره نرفتم هرگز

نومید نیم ز بارگاهِ کرمت

زیراکه یکی را دو نگفتم هرگز

٢٦٩

کردیم دگر شیوهٔ رندی آغاز

تکبیر همی زنیم بر پنج نماز

هر جا که صراحی است مارا بینی

گردن چو صراحی سویِ آن کرده دراز

---

269. C. L. N. A. B. I. J. *Takbír*, the formula " *Allah Akbar*," in saying which the mind should be abstracted from worldly thoughts; hence " renunciation." Nicolas.

270.

We are but chessmen destined, it is plain,
That great chess player Heaven to entertain :
   Us men it moves about the board of life,
Then in the box of death shuts up again.

271.

You ask what is this life so frail, so vain,
'Tis long to tell, yet will I make it plain :
   'Tis but a breath blown from the vasty
     deeps,
And then blown back to those same deeps
     again !

272.

To-day to love and rapture we have soared,
To-day in Magian precincts wine adored,
   And rapt beyond ourselves we do abide
Within that tavern, "Am not I your Lord?"

---

270. L N B *Haqíqatí*, see Bl , Prosody 3.
271. C. L N. A l. J. Some MSS read *naksh*
Deeps. i.e the ocean of Not-being.

۲۷۰

ما لعبتگانیم و فلك لعبت باز

از روی حقیقتی نه از روی مجاز

بازیچه همکنیم بر نطع وجود

رفتیم بصندوق عدم یك يك باز

۲۷۱

میپرسیدی كه چیست این نفس مجاز

گر بر گویم حقیقت‌ش هست دراز

نفسیست پدید آمده از دریائی

و انگاه شده بقعر آن دریا باز

۲۷۲

ما عاشق و آشفته و مستیم امروز

در كوی مغان باده پرستیم امروز

از هستی خویشتن بكلّی رسته

پیوسته بمحراب أَلَسَتیم امروز

---

272. C. L. N. A. I. J. *Alasto birabbikum*, Allah's
words to Adam's sons: Koran, vii. 171. So in Hafiz,
Ode 43 (Brockhaus). Perhaps meant as a parody of Sufi
phraseology.

273.

My queen (long may she live to vex her slave !)
To-day a token of affection gave,

Darting a kind glance from her eyes, she
passed,

And said, " Do good and cast it on the wave ! "

274.

I put my lips to the cup, for I did yearn
The means of gaining length of days to learn :

It leaned its lip to mine, and whispered low,

" Drink ! for, once gone, you never will return. '

275.

Wrapped in the cloak of Naught we slumbered
till

Thou bad'st us wake; this hard world treats
us ill;

And we're bewildered by Thy strange com-
mand,

From slanted jars no single drop to spill.

---

273. L N Meaning, hope not for a return to your
love *Nehíyey*, " a good act. ' *ya* conjunctive and *y i i tankir*.
Vullers, p 250.

۲۷۳

معشوق که عمرش چو غمم باد دراز

امروز بنو تلطّفی کرد آغاز

بر چشم ِ من انداخت دمی چشم و رفت

یعنی که نکوئی کن و در آب انداز

۲۷۴

لب بر لب ِ کوزه بردم از غایت ِ آز

تا زو طلبم واسطهٔ عمر ِ دراز

لب بر لب ِ من نهاد و می گفت براز

می خور که بدین جهان نمی آئی باز

۲۷۵

در کتم ِ عدم خفته بُدم گفتی خیز

دارد بجهان دور ِ جهان شورانگیز

و اکنون که بفرمان ِ تو ام حیرانم

القصّه چنان دار که کج دار و مریز

---

274. C. L. A. B. I. J. Some MSS. give line 4 differently.
275. L. Naught, *i.e.* Not-being. See note to No. 183.
Line 2, literally, "In the world the circling of the troublous
world holds us."

276.

O Thou! who know'st the secret thoughts
　　of all,
In time of sorest need who aidest all,
　Grant me repentance, and accept my plea,
O Thou who dost accept the pleas of all!

277.

At Tús a bird perched in the ruined street,
And on the skull of Kaiús set his feet,
　And made complaint, "Alas, alas, poor king,
Hushed are thy bells, thy drums have ceased to
　　beat."

278.

Ask not the chances of futurity,
Nor grieve for joys that now are lost to thee:
　Set down as gain this ready-money breath!
Forget the past, and let the future be.

276　C. L. N. A I J　Note tashdid on rabb dropped.
Taubadih, "giver of repentance"

277. C L N. A　Tús, near Nishapúr was once the
capital of Persia.　Kaiús, one of the early kings.

٢٧٦

ای واقفِ اسرارِ ضمیرِ همه کس
در حالتِ عجز دستگیرِ همه کس
یا رب تو مرا توبه ده و عُذر پذیر
ای توبه‌ده و عذرپذیرِ همه کس

٢٧٧

مرغی دیدم نشسته بر بارهٔ طوس
در پیش نهاده کلّهٔ کیکاؤس
با کلّه همیگفت که افسوس افسوس
کو بانگِ جرسها و کجا ناله‌ٔ کوس

٢٧٨

از حادثهٔ زمانه آینده مپرس
وز هرچه رسد چو نیست پاینده مپرس
این یکدمه نقد را غنیمت میدان
از رفته میندیش وز آینده مپرس

---

278. C. L. N. A. I. J. In line 1 note *izáfat* dropped after silent *he*. Compare Horace's Ode to Leuconoe: "*Tu ne quæ sieris*," &c. Odes, i. 11.

279.

What launched that golden orb his course to
    run,
What wrecks his firm foundations, when 'tis
    done,
  No man of science ever weighed with scales,
Or made assay with touchstone, no, not one !

280.

Oh, prithee, to my counsel lend thine ear,
Take not on thee hypocrisy's veneer ;
  This life one moment is, the next all time,
Sell not eternity for earthly gear !

281.

Ofttimes I plead my foolishness to Thee,
My heart's contraction and perplexity :
  I gird me with the Magian zone, and why ?
For shame so poor a Musulman to be.

---

279. L. The vanity of science.

280 C L N A. B. I Note *íd* separated from its
noun, as before. Vullers, p. 173.

٢٧٩

آغازِ دوانِ گشتنِ آن زرّینِ طاس

و انجامِ خرابیّ چذین ذیك آساس

دانسته نمیشود بمعیارِ عقول

سنجیده نمیشود بمقیاسِ قیاس

٢٨٠

پندی دهمت اگر بمن داری گوش

از بهرِ خدا جامهٔ تزویر مپوش

عقبیٰ همه ساعتست و دنیا یكدم

از بهرِ دمی ملكِ ابدرا مفروش

٢٨١

تا چند کنم عرضهٔ نادانیِ خویش

بگرفت دلِ من از پریشانیِ خویش

زنّارِ مغانه بر میان خواهم بست

دانی ز چه از ننگِ مسلمانیِ خویش

---

281. C. L N. A. I. J. In line 1 scan *nádáníyí*, dissolving the long *yá*.

282.

Khayyam! rejoice that wine you still can pour,
And still the charms of tulip cheeks adore;

    You'll soon not be, rejoice then that you are.
Think how 't would be in case you were no
    more!

283.

Once, in a potter's shop, a company
Of cups in converse did I chance to see,

    And lo! one lifted up his voice, and cried,
"Who made, who sells, who buys this crockery?"

284.

Last night, as I reeled past the tavern door,
Out came an elder, who a wine-jug bore,

    I said, "O Shaikh, have you no fear of
    God?"
Quoth he, "God hath much mercy in his store.'

---

282   C. L. N. A. B. I. J.

283.   C. L. N. A. B. I. J.   Men's speculations as to their
origin and destiny.

۲۸۲

خیّام اگر ز بادهٔ مستی خوش باش
با لاله رخی اگر نشستی خوش باش
چون آخر کار نیست خواهی بودن
انگار که نیستی چو هستی خوش باش

۲۸۳

در کارگه کوزه‌گری رفتم دوش
دیدم دو هزار کوزه گویا و خموش
ناگاه یکی کوزه بر آورد خروش
کو کوزه‌گر و کوزه‌خر و کوزه فروش

۲۸۴

سرمست بمیخانه گذر کردم دوش
پیری دیدم مست و سبوئی بر دوش
گفتم ز خدا شرم نداری ای پیر
گفنا کرم از خداست رو باده بنوش

---

284 C. L N. A I J Sar mast, a compound, hence
izáfat omitted Saboyé, hamza (on conjunctive yá) followed by yá i tankín. See Lumsden, ıı 269

285.

Life's fount is wine, Khizer its guardian,
I, like Elias, find it where I can ;
    'Tis sustenance for heart and spirit too,
Allah himself calls wine " a boon to man."

286.

Though wine is banned, yet drink, for ever
        drink !
By day and night, with strains of music, drink !
    Where'er thou lightest on a cup of wine,
Spill just one drop, and take the rest, and
        drink !

287.

Although the creeds number some seventy three,
I hold with none but that of love to Thee :
    What matter faith, unfaith, obedience, sin ?
Thou 'rt all we need, the rest is vanity.

---

285 C L N A. I. J. Koran, ii. 216. Elias, or
Khizer, discovered the water of life.

286. C. L N. A. I J. To spill a drop is a sign of

۲۸۵

می را که خضَر خجسته دارد پاسش
او آبِ حیاتست و منم اَلیاسش
من قوّتِ دل و قوتِ روحش خوانم
چون گفت خدا مَنَافِعٌ لِلنَّاسش

۲۸۶

می گرچه حرامست مدامش مینوش
با نغمه و چنگِ صبح و شامش مینوش
جامی ز میِ لعل گرت دست دهد
یک قطره رها کن و تمامش مینوش

۲۸۷

هفتاد و دو مِلّتند در دین کم و بیش
از مِلّتها عشقِ تو دارم در پیش
چه کفر و چه اسلام چه طاعت چه گناه
مقصود توئی بهانه بردار از پیش

---

liberality. Nicolas. *Garat dast dihad*, "If it fall into thy
hand."

287. N. See note on Quatrain 194. Forms of faith
are indifferent. See *Gulshan i Ráz*, p. 83.

288.

Tell one by one my scanty virtues o'er ;
As for my sins, forgive them by the score ;

Let not these trifles fan Thy wrath to flame :
For the dead Prophet's sake, forgive once more !

289.

Grieve not at coming ill, you can't defeat it,
It adds to grief to look ahead to meet it ;

Take heart ! let not the world depress you so,
Your fate is fixed, and grieving will not cheat it.

290.

There is a chalice made with art profound,
And with its Maker's approbation crowned ;

Yet the world's Potter takes his masterpiece,
And dashes it to pieces on the ground !

---

288. L N. B Also ascribed to Zahír ud-din Faryábi
(d 598 A.H)   M.   Az bád i haica means " without cause"
as well as " wind."

٢٨٨

یك یك هنرم ببین و گنه ده ده بخش

هر جرم که رفت حسبةً للّه بخش

از بادِ هوا آتـشِ کین را مفروز

ما را بسرِ خاكِ رَسُولُ اللّه بخش

٢٨٩

غم چند خوری ز کارِ نا آمده پیش

رنجست نصیب مردمِ دوراندیش

خوش باش و جهان تنگ مکن بر دلِ خویش

کز خوردنِ غم قضا نگردد کم و بیش

٢٩٠

جامیست که عقلِ آفرین می زندش

صد بوسه ز مهٔر بر جبین می زندش

این کوزه گرِ دهٔر چنین جامِ لطیف

می سازد و باز بر زمین می زندش

289. L.

290. C. L. A. I. J. So Job: "Is it good unto Thee
that Thou shouldest despise the labour of Thine hands?"

291.

In truth wine is a spirit thin as air,
A limpid soul in the cup's earthen ware;
  No dull dense person shall be friend of mine
Save wine-cups, which are dense and also rare.

292.

O wheel of heaven! no ties of bread you feel,
No ties of salt, you flay me like an eel!
  A woman's wheel spins clothes for man and
      wife,
It does more good than you, O heavenly wheel!

293.

If roses fail I'll deck me with a thorn,
And welcome darkness if of light forlorn;
  And if I lose my prayer-mats, beads, and
      Shaikh,
Those Christian bells and stoles I will not scorn.

---

291 L N. B *Láyiq* . . . *man* *izáfat* omitted
because of the intervening words. Lumsden, ii., 250
292. C L N. A I J.

٢٩١

می در قدحِ انصاف که جانیست لطیف
در کالبدِ شیشه روانیست لطیف
لایـق نبُوَد هیچ گران همدم من
جز ساغرِ باده کان گرانیست لطیف

٢٩٢

ای چرخِ فلک نه نان شناسی نه نمک
پیوسته مرا برَهنه سازی چو سمک
از چرخِ زنی دو شخص پوشیده شود
پس چرخِ زنی به از تو ای چرخِ فلک

٢٩٣

گر گل نبُوَد نصیبِ ما خار اینک
ور نور بما نمیرسد تار اینک
ور سبحه و سجّاده و شیخی نبُوَد
ناقوس و کلیسیا و زنّار اینک

---

293.   C. L. N. A. I. (under *Te*).   So Pope:
"For forms and creeds let graceless zealots fight,
   He can't be wrong whose life is in the right."
See my translation of the *Masnavi*, p. 82.

294.

"If heaven deny me peace and fame," I said,
"Let it be open war and shame instead;
   Let him who scorns bright purple wine
      beware,
I'll arm me with a stone, and break his head!"

295.

See! the dawn breaks, and rends night's canopy:
Arise! and drain a morning draught with me!
   Away with gloom! full many a dawn will
      break
Looking for us, and we not here to see!

296.

Thou who regardest not the fires of hell,
Nor seekest cleansing at contrition's well,
   When winds of death shall quench thy vital
      torch,
Beware lest earth thy guilty dust expel.

---

294. C L N. A. I. J.
295 C. L N. A. I. J. *Bisyâr*, "frequently"

۲۹۴

گر صلح نیابم ز فلک جنگ اینک
ور نام نکو نباشدم ننگ اینک
جام می لعل ارغوان رنگ اینک
آنکس که نمیخورد سر و سنگ اینک

۲۹۵

هین صبح دمید و دامن شب شد چاک
برخیز و صبوح کن چرائی غمناک
می نوش دلا که صبح بسیار دمد
او روی بما کرده و ما روی بخاک

۲۹۶

از آتش آخرت نمیداری باک
در آب ندامت نشدی هرگز پاک
چون باد اجل چراغ عمرت بکُشد
ترسم که ترا ز ننگ نپذیرد خاک

---

296. L. Possibly written by some pious reader as an
answer to Khayyam's scoffs. See note on Quatrain 223.

297.

This world an insubstantial pageant deem ;
All wise men know things are not what they
    seem ;
  Be of good cheer, and drink, and so shake off
This vain illusion of a baseless dream.

298.

Find one of cypress stature, fresh and fair
As new-blown rose, thy daily cups to share,
  Ere blast of death tear off thy robe of life,
Like the dead rose leaves lying scattered there !

299.

Be not a prey to care and idle pother,
But bumpers drain the livelong year, O brother ;
  Yea, dally with the daughter of the grape,
She's naughty, but she's nicer than the mother !

---

297. L N. All earthly existence is "*Maya*," as the
Hindoos say.

298. C. L. N. A. I. J. The Lucknow commentator

٢٩٧

این صورتِ کونِ جمله نقشست و خیال

عارف نبُوَد هر که ندارد این حال

بنشین قدحِ باده بنوش و خوشباش

فارغ شو ازین نقش و خیالاتِ محال

٢٩٨

با سرو قدی تازه‌تر از خرمنِ گل

از دست مده جامِ می و دامنِ گل

زان پیش که ناگه شود از بادِ اجل

پیراهنِ عمرِ تو چو پیراهنِ گل

٢٩٩

در سر مگذار هیچ سودای محال

می خور همه سال ساغرِ مالامال

با دخترِ رز نشین و عیشی میکن

دختر حرام به که مادر بحلال

---

says *dáman i gul* means the maid's cheek.

299. N. "Daughter of the grape," *i.e.* wine, a translation of an Arabic phrase.

300.

My love shone forth, and I was overcome,
My heart was speaking, but my tongue was
    dumb ;
   Beside the water-brooks I died of thirst.
Was ever known so strange a martyrdom?

301.

Give me my cup in hand, and sing a glee
In concert with the bulbuls' symphony ;
   Wine would not gurgle as it leaves the flask,
If drinking mute were right for thee and me !

302.

The "Truth" will not be shown to lofty thought,
Nor yet with lavished gold may it be bought :
   Till self be mortified for fifty years,
From words to "states of heart" no soul is
    brought.

---

300   N   *Dil rubáyé*, "that well-known charmer."
Lumsden, ii 142   *Pur sukhan*, "full of speech"
  301. C. L. N A 1. J.
  302. L. line 3, literally, "Unless you dig up your

٣٠٠

عشقی بکمال و دلربائی بجمال
دل پر سخن و زبان ز گفتن شده لال
زین نادره ترکه دید یا رب بجهان
من تشنه و پیش من روان آب زلال

٣٠١

می بر کف من نه و بر آور غلغل
با نالهٔ عندلیب و صوت بلبل
بی نغمه اگر روا بُدی می خوردن
می از سر شیشه مینکردی قلقل

٣٠٢

اسرار حقیقت نشود حل بسوال
نه نیز به درباختن نعمت و مال
تا جان نکنی و خون خوری پنجه سال
از قال ترا ره نه نمایند بحال

---

soul, and eat blood for fifty years." 'States' of ecstatic
union with the 'Truth,' or Deity of the Mystics, and
intuition of Him by the "eye of certainty." See my
translation of the *Masnavi*, p. 166.

303.

I solved all problems, down from Saturn's
    wreath
Unto this lowly sphere of earth beneath,
    And leapt out free from bonds of fraud
        and lies,
Yea, every knot was loosed, save that of death!

304.

Peace! the eternal "Has been" and "To be '
Pass man's experience, and man's theory;
    Now is the time for joy; naught equals wine,
To all these riddles wine supplies the key!

305.

Allah, our Lord, is merciful, though just;
Sinner! despair not, but His mercy trust!
    For though to-day you perish in your sins,
To-morrow He'll absolve your crumbling dust.

---

303. C. L A I. J   Ascribed to Avicenna (Ethé, No 3).
Saturn's rings unknown to Omar, but demands of rhyme
inexorable. *Hama, Har*, &c., often written without *izáfat*

٣٠٣

از جرمِ حضيضِ خاك تا اوجِ زحل
كردم همه مشكلاتِ گردون را حل
بيرون جَستم ز بندِ هر مكّر و حيل
هر سَدّ كشاده شد مگر بندِ اجَل

٣٠٤

تا كى ز ابد حديث و تا كى ز ازل
بگْذشت ز اندازهٔ من علم و عمل
هنگامِ طرب شراب را نيست بَدَل
هر مشكل را شراب گرداند حل

٣٠٥

از خالقِ كردگار و از ربِّ رحيم
نوميد مشو بجرمِ عصيانِ عظيم
گر مست و خراب مرده باشى امروز
فردا بخشد بر استخوانهاىِ رميم

Lumsden, ii. 249, see Bl., Prosody, 12.

  304. C. L. A. B. I. J.

  305. C. L. N. A. I. J. A very Voltairean quatrain.

306.

Your course annoys me, O ye wheeling skies!
Unloose me from your chain of tyrannies!
 If none but fools your favours may enjoy,
Then favour me,—I am not very wise!

307.

O City Mufti, you go more astray
Than I, although to drinking I give way;
 I drink the blood of grapes, you that of men:
Which of us is the more bloodthirsty, pray?

308.

Fill up the cup! nor brood eternally
On what is past, and what is yet to be;
 Our prisoned spirits, lent us for a day,
A while from reason's bondage let us free!

---

306. C. L. N A I J. H. has one somewhat similar
307. C. L. N A I. J. Alluding to the selling of justice
by Muftis.

٣۰٦

ای چرخ ز گردشِ تو خرسند نیم

آزادم کن که لایقِ بند نیم

گر میلِ تو با بیخرد و نادانست

من نیز چنان اهل و خردمند نیم

٣۰۷

ای مفتیِ شهْر از تو پر کارتریم

با این همه مستی از تو هشیارتریم

تو خونِ کسان خوری و ما خونِ رزان

انصاف بده کدام خونخوارتریم

٣۰۸

آن به که بجامِ بادهِ دل شاد کنیم

وز آمده و گذشته کم یاد کنیم

وین عاریتی روانِ زندانی‌را

یکلحظه ز بندِ عقل آزاد کنیم

308. C. L. N. A. I. J. 'Āriyatī rawán, " this borrowed soul."

309.

When Khayyam quittance at Death's hand
    receives,
And sheds his outworn life, as trees their leaves,
    Full gladly will he sift this world away,
Ere dustmen sift his ashes in their sieves.

310.

This wheel of heaven, whereat we're all
    dismayed,
I liken to a lamp's revolving shade,
    The sun the candlestick, the earth the shade,
And men the trembling forms thereon portrayed.

311.

Who was it that did knead my clay? Not I.
Who spun my web of silk and wool? Not I.
    Who wrote upon my forehead all my good
And all my evil deeds? In truth, not I.

---

309. C L. N. A I. J
310. C. N. A. B I. *Fánús i khıyál*, a magic or Chinese
lantern.

٣٠٩

آن لحظه که از اجل گریزان گردم
چون برگ ز شاخ عمر ریزان گردم
عالم بنشاط دل بغربال کنیم
زان پیش که خاک خاکبیزان گردم

٣١٠

این چرخ فلک که ما درو حیرانیم
فانوس خیال ازو مثالی دانیم
خورشید چراغدان و عالم فانوس
ما چون صُوَریم کاندر او گردانیم

٣١١

از آب و گلم سرشته‌ء من چکنم
وین پشم و قصب تو رشته‌ء من چکنم
هر نیک و بدی که آید از ما بوجود
تو بر سر من نوشته‌ء من چکنم

---

311. C. L. N. A. I. In line 2 the rhyme shows the
word to be *rishtai*, not *rushtai*.

P

312.

O let us not forecast to-morrow's fears,

But count to-day as gain, my brave compeers !

　To-morrow we shall quit this inn, and march

With comrades who have marched seven thou-

　　sand years.

313.

Ne'er for one moment leave your cup unused !

Wine keeps heart, faith, and reason too, amused;

　Had Iblis swallowed but a single drop,

To worship Adam he had ne'er refused !

314.

Come, dance ! while we applaud thee, and adore

Thy wild Narcissus eyes, and drink the more ;

　A score of cups is no such great affair,

But 'tis enchanting when we reach three score !

---

312   C L N A I J   Badáúni (ii 337) says the creation
of Adam was 7000 years before his time   Compare Hafiz,
Rubá'i, 10 (Brockhaus, No 625), and Horace, Ode to
Plancus, i 7.

۳۱۲

ای دوست بیا تا غم فردا نخوریم
وین یکدمه عمر را غنیمت شمریم
فردا که ازین دیر کهن در گذریم
با هفتهزار سالگان هم سفریم

۳۱۳

بی باده مباش تا توانی یکدم
کز باده شود عقل و دل و دین خرّم
ابلیس اگر باده بخوردی یکدم
کردی دو هزار سجده پیش آدم

۳۱۴

بر خیز و بکوب پای تا دست زنیم
مَی در نظر نرگس سر مست زنیم
در بیست زدن ذوق ندارد چندان
ذوق عجب آن بود که درشت زنیم

---

313. C. L. (in part) N. A. I. J. See Koran. ii. 31.

314. N. Line 2, "drink wine in the view of thy intoxi-
cating eyes." The play on *Zaném* cannot be reproduced.

315.

I close the suitor's door in my own face,
And ask no aid from noble or from base!
  I have but ONE to lend a helping hand,
He knows, as well as I, my sorry case.

316.

Ah! by these heavens, that ever circling run,
And by my own base lusts I am undone;
  I lack the wisdom to renounce the world,
And the discretion its allures to shun.

317.

On earth's green carpet many sleepers lie.
And hid beneath it others I descry;
  And others, not yet come, or passed away,
People the desert of Nonentity!

---

315   C. L N A I. J.   A "*Háliya*" quatrain, lament-
ing his own condition   *Chunánki hastam hastam,* " how I
am, (yea) how I am."

۳۱۵

بر خود درِ کام و آرزو در بستم
وز منّتِ هر ناکس و کس وا رستم
جز دوست چو کس نیست که گیرد دستم
من دانم و او چنانکه هستم هستم

۳۱۶

پیوسته ز گردشِ فلک غمگینم
با طبعِ خسیسِ خویشتن در کینم
علمی نه که از سرِ جهان بر خیزم
عقلی نه که فارغ ز جهان بنشینم

۳۱۷

بر مفرشِ خاک خفتگان می بینم
در زیرِ زمین نهفتگان می بینم
چندانکه بصحرایِ عدم مینگرم
نا آمدگان و رفتگان می بینم

316. C. L. N. A. I. J.

317. C. L. N. A. I. J. The sleepers on the earth are
those sunk in the sleep of superstition and ignorance.

318.

Sure of Thy grace, for sins why need I fear?
How can the pilgrim faint whilst Thou art near?
　　On the last day Thy grace will wash me white,
And all my " black record " will disappear.

319.

Think not I dread from out the world to hie.
And see my disembodied spirit fly;
　　I tremble not at death, for death is true,
'Tis my ill life that makes me fear to die !

320.

Let us shake off dull reason's incubus,
No more our tale of days or years discuss.
　　But take our jugs, and plenish them with
　　　　wine,
Or e'er grim potters make their jugs of us!

318　C. L N A. I J　Am is usual after silent he, not
after naw. Lumsden, n 72. See Koran, xin 47.
　319　C. L N. A 1 J　'Death is true,' i.e a certainty.
So Sir Philip Sidney (after M Aurelius) :

۳۱۸

با رحمتِ تو من از گنه نااندیشم
با توشهٴ تو ز رنجِ ره نااندیشم
گر لطفِ تو ام سفیدرو کرداند
یک ذرّه زَ نامهٴ سیه نااندیشم

۳۱۹

تا ظن نبری که از جهان میترسم
وز مردن و از رفتنِ جان میترسم
مردن چو حقیقتست زان باکم نیست
چون نیک نزیستم ازان میترسم

۳۲۰

تا چند اسیرِ عقلِ هر روزه شویم
در دهرچه صد ساله چه یکروزه شویم
در ده تو بکاسه می ازان پیش که ما
در کارگهِ کوزهگران کوزه شویم

" Since Nature's works be good, and death doth serve
As Nature's work, why should we fear to die ? "

320.   C. L. N. A. B. I. J.   *Har roza*, an adjective.

321.

How much more wilt thou chide, O raw divine,
For that I drink, and am a libertine ?
    Thou hast thy weary beads, and saintly show,
Leave me my lively sweetheart, and my wine !

322.

Against my lusts I ever war, in vain.
I think on my ill deeds with shame and pain :
    I trust Thou wilt assoil me of my sins,
But, even so, the shame must still remain.

323.

In these twin compasses, O Love, you see
One body with two heads, like you and me,
    Which wander round one centre, circlewise.
But at the last in one same point agree.

321. C L. N. A. I. J.
322   C. L N. A. B I II.
323. C. L. N. A. I. FitzGerald quotes a similar conceit

۳۲۱

تا چند ملامت کنی ای زاهدِ خام

ما رندِ خراباتی و مستیم مدام

تو در غمِ تسبیح و ریا و تلبیس

ما با می و معشوقه مداميم بكام

۳۲۲

با نفس همیشه در نبردم چکنم

وز کردهٴ خویشتن بدردم چکنم

گیرم که ز من در گذرانی بکرم

زان شرم که دیدی که چه کردم چکنم

۳۲۳

جانا من و تو نمونهٴ پرگاریم

سر گرچه دو کرده ایم یکتن داریم

بر نقطه روانیم کنون دائره وار

تا آخرِ کار سر بهم باز آزیم

---

used by the poet Donne, for which see Ward's "English
Poets," i. 562. The two heads are the points of the compasses.

324.

We shall not stay here long, but while we do,
'Tis folly wine and sweethearts to eschew;
　　Why ask if earth etern or transient be?
Since you must go, it matters not to you.

325.

In reverend sort to mosque I wend my way,
But, by great Allah, it is not to pray;
　　No, but to steal a prayer-mat! When 'tis
　　　　worn,
I go again, another to purvey.

326.

Be not cast down by fickle Fortune's spite,
But quaff your wine rose-hued and sparkling
　　　　bright;
　　The world's our murderer, and wine its blood,
To drink that blood is only meet and right!

---

324. C. L N. A. B I J.
325. C L N A. B. I. J.　To "steal a prayer-mat," is

۳۲۴

چون نیست مقام ما دریں دیر مقیم

پس بی می و معشوق خطائیست عظیم

تا کی ز قدیم و محدث ای مردِ حکیم

چون من رفتم جهان چه محدث چه قدیم

۳۲۵

در مسجد اگرچه با نیاز آمده ام

حقّا که نه از بهر نماز آمده ام

روزی اینجا سجّادهٔ دزدیدم

آن کهنه شدست باز باز آمده ام

۳۲۶

دیگر غمِ ایں گردشِ گردون نخوریم

جز بادهٔ ذابِ صافِ گلگون نخوریم

می خونِ جهانست و جهان خونیِ ما

ما خونِ دلِ خونیِ خود چون نخوریم

to pray to be seen of men.—Nicolas. A satire on some
hypocrite, perhaps himself.

326. L. N. See Koran, ii. 187.

327

For Thy dear sake I'll cast repute away,
And, if I break my vow, the fine will pay;
　　Life is too small a sacrifice; I'd bear
Thy cruelty e'en till the judgment day.

328.

In Being's round we find ourselves belated,
And manhood's honour humbled and abated;
　　This life responds not to the heart's desire,—
Away with it, for with it we are sated!

329.

The world is tricksome, I'll play tricks as well,
And with bright wine and gladness ever dwell!
　　They say, " May Allah grant thee penitence !"
He grants it not, and did he, I'd rebel !

---

327. C L N. A. B I. Note *izáfat* dropped after silent
he, and *rá* separated from its noun.
328. L N.

۳۲۷

در عشقِ تو صد گونه ملامت بکشم

ور بشکنم این عهد غرامت بکشم

گر عمر وفا کند جفاهایِ ترا

باری کم ازانکه تا قیامت بکشم

۳۲۸

در دایرهٔ وجود دیر آمده ایم

وز پایهٔ مردمی بزیر آمده ایم

چون عمر نه بر مرادِ ما میگذرد

ای کاش سر آمدی که سیر آمده ایم

۳۲۹

دنیا چو فناست من بجز فن نکنم

جز یادِ نشاط و میِ روشن نکنم

گویند مرا که ایزدت توبه دهاد

او خود ندهد ور بدهد من نکنم

---

329. C. L. N. A. B. I. J. Note the pun on *faná*, 'illusion' and *fan* 'art, fraud.'

330.

When Death shall tread me down and pluck me
    bare
Of this brave plumage which through life I wear,
    Then mould me to a cup and fill with wine,—
Its bouquet will revive me then and there !

331.

So far as this world's dealings I have traced,
I find its favours shamefully misplaced ;
    Allah be praised that I am one of those
Who 're disappointed by it and disgraced !

332.

'Tis dawn ! my heart with wine I will recruit,
And dash to bits the glass of good repute ;
    All my long-cherished hopes I will renounce,
Play with long tresses and attune the lute.

---

330. C L N A. B I J. *Parkanda*, 'plucked' (as a
fowl).
331. C. L N. A. I '*Alam kama*, &c, "states entirely

۳۳۰

در پایِ اجل چو من سرافگنده شوم
در دستِ اجل چو مرغ پرکنده شوم
زینهار گِلم بجز صراحی مکنید
باشد که ببویِ می دمی زنده شوم

۳۳۱

زین گونه که من کارِ جهان میبینم
عالم همه رایگان بران می بینم
سبحان الله بهر چه در مینگرم
ناکامیِ خویش اندر آن می بینم

۳۳۲

صبح است دمی بر میِ گلرنگی زنیم
وین شیشهءِ نام وننگ بر سنگی زنیم
دست از املِ درازِ خود باز کشیم
در زلفِ درازِ و دامنِ چنگی زنیم

gratuitous." Write *barán* without a *madd.* Bl., Prosody,
p. 11. Compare Shakespeare, Sonnet 66.

332. L. N. B.

333.

Though I had sinned the sins of all mankind,
I know Thou wouldst to mercy be inclined;
   Thou sayest, " I will help in time of need :"
One more in need than me where wilt Thou find ?

334.

Am I a wine-bibber?   What if I am ?
A giaour, or infidel?   Suppose I am ?
   Each sect miscalls me, but I heed them not,
I am my own, and, what I am, I am.

335.

All my life long to drink I've never ceased,
And drink I will to-night on Kader's feast ;
   And throw my arms about the wine-jar's neck,
And kiss its lip, and clasp it to my breast !

---

333   C. L N A. I. J   The *waw* in *'afw* is a consonant, and therefore takes *kasra* for the *izáfat*, without the intervention of euphonic *yá*. Abu Su'íd has a quatrain ending with two similar lines   (Ethé, No 11)

۳۳۳

گر من ز گندهِ رويِ زمين کردستم

عفوِ تو اميد است که گيرد دستم

گفتی که بروزِ عجز دستت گيرم

عاجزتر ازين مخواه کاکنون هستم

۳۳۴

گر من ز مىِ مغانه مستم هستم

ور کافر و گبر و بت پرستم هستم

هر طائفه ء بمن گمانى دارند

من زانِ خودم چنانکه هستم هستم

۳۳۵

هشيار نبوده ام دمى تا هستم

امشب شب قدرست و من امشب مستم

لب بر لبِ جام و سينه بر سينهء خم

تا روز بگردنِ صراحى دستم

334. C. L. N. A. I. J. *Zan i khud* for *azán i khud*, "my own property."

335. C. L. N. A. I. J. *Kadr*, the night of power. Koran, xcvi. 1.

336.

Being and Notbeing alike I know,
Essence of things above and things below,
    But,—shame upon my knowledge!—to be
        drunk
Is after all the highest lore I know.

337.

Though I drink wine, I am no libertine,
Nor am I grasping, save of cups of wine;
    You ask me why I worship wine?   Because
To worship self, like you, I still decline.

338.

To confidants like you I dare to say
What mankind really are:—moulded of clay,
    Affliction's clay, and kneaded in distress,
They taste the world awhile, then pass away

---

336   L N. B
337   C L N A. I J. A hit at the vain and covetous
Mollas   Also ascribed to Anwari (d about 587)   M

۳۳٦

من ظاهرِ نیستی و هستی دانم
من باطنِ هر فراز و پستی دانم
با اینهمه از دانشِ خود شرمم باد
گر مرتبهٔء ورایِ مستی دانم

۳۳۷

من باده خورم و لیک مستی نکنم
الّا بقدح درازدستی نکنم
دانی غرضم ز می پرستی چه بود
تا همچو تو خویشتن پرستی نکنم

۳۳۸

محرم هستی که با تو گویم یك دم
کز اوّل کار خود چه بودست آدم
محنت زدهٔء سرشته اندر گلِ غم
یکچند جهان بخورْد و برداشت قدم

339.

We make the wine-jar's lip our place of prayer,
And drink in lessons of true manhood there,
   And pass our lives in taverns, if perchance
The time misspent in mosques we may repair.

340.

Man is the whole creation's summary,
The apple, as it were, of wisdom's eye ;
   The circle of existence is a ring,
Whereof the signet is humanity.

341.

With fancies, as with wine, our heads we turn,
Aspire to heaven, and earthly trammels spurn :
   But, when we drop this fleshly clog, 'tis seen
From dust we came, and back to dust return.

---

339. L N In line 4 scan *sawmä'älä*. This quatrain
is probably mystical.

340. C. L N. A. I In line 3 scan *angashtäriyast.*

٣٣٩

ما جايِ نمازی بلبِ خم کردیم

خود را بمی لعل چو مردم کردیم

در کویِ خرابات مگر بتّوان یافت

آن عُمْر که در صومعها گم کردیم

٣٤٠

مقصود ز جمله آفرینش مائیم

در چشمِ خرد جوهرِ بینش مائیم

این دائرهٔ جهان چو انگشتری است

بی هیچ شکی نقشِ نگینش مائیم

٣٤١

ما کز می بیخودی طربناک شدیم

وز پایهٔ دون بر سرِ افلاك شدیم

آخر همه ز الایشِ تن پاك شدیم

از خاك بر آمدیم و با خاك شدیم

Man is the microcosm. See *Gulshan i Ráz*, p. 15. "The captain jewel of the carcanet."

341. L. N.

312.

If it be true that I did break the fast,
Think not I meant it; no! I thought 'twas
    past ;—
   That day more weary than a sleepless night,—
And blessèd breakfast-time had come at last !

343.

That cup of joy I never drank at all,
Wherein was mingled none of sorrow's gall ;
   Nor ever dipped my hand in pleasure's sauce,
But pain soon came and made me smart withal.

344.

At dawn to tavern haunts I wend my way,
And with distraught Kalandars pass the day ;
   O Thou to whom all secret things are known,
Grant me Thy grace, that I may learn to pray !

312. L. N. *Roza khwandan*, " to avoid fasting " In
line 2, for *bekhabar* read *bákhabar*.
343. C. L. N A. I. Line 4, literally, " eat a roast of

۳۴۲

من در رمضان روزه اگر میخوردم

تا ظنّ نبری که با خبر میخوردم

از محنتِ روزه روزِ من چون شب بود

پنداشته بودم که سحر میخوردم

۳۴۳

هرگز بطرب شربتِ آبی نخوریم

تا از کفِ اندوه شرابی نخوریم

نانی نـزنیم در نمك هیچ گهی

تا از جگرِ خویش کبابی نخوریم

۳۴۴

هر روز پگاه در خرابات شوم

همراهِ قلندرانِ طامات شوم

چون عالمِ سرّ و لخفیّات توئی

توفیقم ده تا بمناجات شوم

my own liver."

344. C. L. N. A. I. J. Kalandars, *i.e.* religious men-
dicants of doubtful repute. See *Gulistán*, viii. 32.

315.

These worldly cares I rate not at one grain,
So I eat once a day, I don't complain;
 And, since earth's kitchen yields no solid food.
I pester no man with petitions vain. ·

346.

Never from worldly toils have I been free,
Never for one short moment glad to be !
 I served a long apprenticeship to fate.
But yet of fortune gained no mastery.

347.

One hand with Koran, one with wine-cup dight.
I half incline to wrong, and half to right;
 This azure crystal dome beholds in me
A sorry Moslem, yet not heathen quite.

---

345. C. L. N. A I J. In line 3 the *Aly* in *az* is not treated as an *Aly i wasl.* Bl Pros, 10

۳۴۵

یك جو غمِ ایّامِ نداریم خوشیم

گر چاشت بود شام نداریم خوشیم

چون پختهٔ بما نمیرسد از مطبخ

از کس طمعِ خام نداریم خوشیم

۳۴۶

یك روز ز بندِ عالم آزاد نیم

یك دم زدن از وجودِ خود شاد نیم

شاگردیِ روزگار کردم بسیار

در دورِ جهان هنوز استاد نیم

۳۴۷

یك دست بمصحفیم و یکدست بجام

گه نـزدِ حلالیم وگهی نـزدِ حرام

ماثیم درین گنبدِ فیروزهٔ خام

نی کافرِ مطلق نه مسلمانِ تمام

---

346 C. L. N A I. J. *Yak dam zadan,* 'For one
moment'

347 C L N A I. J " *Video meliora proboque,*" &c

348.

Khayyam's respects to Mustafa convey,
And with due reverence ask him to say,

    Why it has pleased him to forbid pure wine,
When he allows his people acid whey ?

349.

Tell Khayyam, for a master of the schools,
He strangely misinterprets my plain rules ;

    Where have I said that wine is wrong for all ?
'Tis lawful for the wise, but not for fools.

350.

My critics call me a philosopher,
But Allah knows full well they greatly err ;

    I know not even what I am, much less
What is the reason that I sojourn here !

---

348 and 349. L and in Whalley's Moradabad edition
Mustafa, i e. Muhammad See Renan, Averroes, 171 . and
Sale's Koran, Prelim. Discourse, Sect. 5

۳۴۸

از من بر مصطفی رسانید سلام

و انگاه بگوئید باعزازِ تمام

کای سیّدِ هاشمی چرا دوغِ ترش

در شرع حلالست و مِی ناب حرام

۳۴۹

از من بر خیّام رسانید سلام

و انگاه بگوئید که خامی خیّام

من کی گفتم که می حرامست ولی

بر پخته حلالست و بر خام حرام

۳۵۰

دشمن بغلط گفت که من فلسفیَم

ایزد داند که آنچه او گفت نیَم

لیکن چو درین غم آشیان آمده ام

آخر کم از آن که من ندانم که کیَم

---

350. C. L. A. I. J. *Filsafat* meant the Greek philosophy
as cultivated by Persian rationalists, in opposition to
theology. Renan, Averroes, p. 91. Compare Montaigne,
" Que scais-je ? "

351.

The more I die to self, I live the more,
The more abase myself, the higher soar :
 And, strange ! the more I drink of Being's
  wine
More sane I grow, and sober than before !

.

352.

Quoth rose, " I am the Yusuf flower, I sweai,
For in my mouth rich golden gems I bear : "
 I said, " Show me another proof. " Quoth she,
" Behold this blood-stained vesture that I wear ! "

353.

I studied with the masters long ago,
And then myself taught pupils what I know :
 Hear now the sum and upshot of it all,—
" We come from earth and to the winds we go."

---

351. L. Clearly mystical. See *Gulshan i Raz*,
Answer xiv.

352. L B. Yusuf is the type of manly beauty The
yellow stamens are compared to his teeth. So Jámí, in

۳۵۱

چندانکه ز خود نیستـترم هستـترم
هرچند بلند پایهتر پستـترم
زین طرفـهتر آنکه از شرابِ هستی
هر لحظه که هشیارترم مستـترم

۳۵۲

گل گفت که من یوسفِ مصرِ چمنم
یاقوتِ گران مایهء پر زر دهنم
گفتم چو تو یوسفی نشانی بنمای
گفتا که بخون غرق مگر پیرهنم

۳۵۳

یکچند بکودکی باستاد شدیم
یکچند باستادیِ خود شاد شدیم
پایانِ سخن شنو که مارا چه رسید
از خاک بر آمدیم و بر باد شدیم

" Yúsuf wa Zulaikha."

353. L. B. FitzGerald compares the dying exclamation of Nizám ul-Mulk, "I am going in the hands of the wind!" *Mantiq ut Tair*, l. 4620

351.

Death finds us soiled, though we were pure at
>> birth,
With grief we go, although we came with
>> mirth ;
>> Watered with tears, and burned with fires
>> of woe,
And, casting life to winds, we rest in earth !

355.

To find great Jamshed's world-reflecting bowl
I compassed sea and land, and viewed the whole ,
>> But, when I asked the wary sage, I learned
That bowl was my own body, and my soul !

356

O wanton Queen, you did intoxicate
And make me pawn who was a knight of late :
>> With bishop and with king you pressed me
>> hard,
And when I meant to castle cried, ' Checkmate !"

---

351   C L A I J.

355   L   King Jamshed's cup, which reflected the
whole world, is the Holy Grail of Persian poetry   Meaning, man is the microcosm.   See note on No 340   In line

٣٥٤

پاك از عدم آمدیم ناپاك شدیم
آسوده در آمدیم و غمناك شدیم
بودیم ز آبِ دیده در آتشِ دل
دادیم بباد عُمر و در خاك شدیم

٣٥٥

در جستنِ جامِ جم جهان پیمودیم
روزی ذه نشستیم و شبی ذه غنودیم
ز استاد چو وصفِ جامِ جم بشنودیم
خود جامِ جهان نمایِ جم ما بودیم

٣٥٦

فرزین مفتا كه مست غمهات شدم
از اسپ پیاده از جفاهات شدم
ز بازیِ فیل و شاه چون در ماندم
رخ بر رخِ تو نهاده ام مات شدم

<hr />

2 scan *naghnádem*

356 C L A. I J. The pun on *rukh*, 'cheek' and
rukh 'castle' is untranslatable. The readings in line 1
seem doubtful.

357.

If Allah wills me not to will aright,
How *can* I frame my will to will aright?

Each single act I will must needs be wrong.
Since none but He *can* make me will aright.

358.

"For once, while roses are in bloom," I said,
"I'll break the law, and please myself instead.

With blooming youths, and maidens' tulip
cheeks
The plain shall blossom like a tulip-bed."

359.

Think not I am existent of myself,
Or walk this blood-stained pathway of myself:

This being is not mine, it is of Him.
Pray what, and where, and whence is this
'myself'?

---

357. C L. A. I J   A *reductio ad absurdum* of the predestination theory

358. L N   *Ro-i, ya i batim* or *tankh*. (?) See note on
No 199

۳۵۷

ایزد چو نخواست آنچه من خواسته ام

کی گردد راست آنچه من خواسته ام

گر جمله صوابست که او خواسته است

پس جمله خطاست آنچه من خواسته ام

۳۵۸

هنگام گلست اختیاری بکنم

و انگه بخلاف شرع کاری بکنم

با سبزه خطان و لاله رخ روزی چند

بر سبزه ز جرعه لاله زاری بکنم

۳۵۹

تا ظن نبری که من بخود موجودم

یا این ره خون خواره بخود پیمودم

این بود نبود من ز بود او بود

من خود که بُدم کجا بُدم کی بودم

---

359. C. L. A. I. J. For *búd u nabúd* I read *búd i nabúd
i man*, "My non-real being is from His being." To say "My
non-being is of His being" seems nonsense.

360.

Endure this world without my wine I cannot !
Drag on life's load without my cups I cannot !
    I'm slave of that sweet moment when they
        say,
" Prithee, take one more goblet," and I cannot !

361.

You, who both day and night the world pursue,
And thoughts of that dread day of doom eschew,
    Bethink you of your latter end ; be sure
As time has treated others, so 'twill you !

362.

O man, who art creation's summary,
Getting and spending weigh too much with thee !
    Arise, and quaff the Etern Cupbearer's wine.
And so from cares about both worlds be free!

---

360   C. L A I J
361   C. L N. A I.
362   C L. N. A I. J. So Wordsworth, " The world is
too much with us," &c   The Sufis rejected *talab ud dunya*,

۳٦۰

من بی می ناب زیستن نتّوانم
بی باده کشید بار تن نـتوانم
من بندهٔ آن دمم که ساقی گوید
یك جام دگر بگیر و من نـتوانم

۳٦۱

ای گشته شب و روز بدنیا نـگران
اندیشه نمیکنی تو از روز گران
آخر نفسی ببین و باز آی بخود
کایّام چگونه میکند با دگران

۳٦۲

ای آنکه توئی خلاصهٔ کون و مکان
بگَذار دهی وسوسهٔ سود و زیان
یکجام می از ساقی باقی بستان
تا باز رهی از غم این هر دو جهان

" worldliness," and *talab ul Ukharat*, " other-worldliness,"
for *talab ul Maula*, " disinterested Godliness." So Madame
Guyon and Fénélon.

363.

From the long circuits of the heavenly zone
Two classes profit reap, and two alone ;
    One studies earthly good and earthly ill,
One heeds not earth's concerns, nor yet its own

364.

Make light to me the world's oppressive weight,
And hide from men my faults and sorry state ,
    And grant me peace to-day, and on the
        morrow
Deal with me as Thy mercy may dictate.

365.

Souls that are well acquaint with this world's
        state,
Its weal and woe with equal mind await,
    For, be it weal we meet, or be it woe,
The weal doth pass, and woe too hath its date.

---

363. C L N A. I. J. Line 2, " Know satisfaction
(belongs to) two classes," i e worldlings and ascetics So
No. 99, line 3. *Tamám,* " entirely "

۳٦۳

از گردشِ این دایرهٔ بی پایان

برخورداری دو نوعِ مردم را دان

یا با خبری تمام از نیك و بدش

یا بیخبری از خود و از کارِ جهان

۳٦۴

احوالِ جهان بر دلم آسان میکن

وافعالِ بدم ز خلق پنهان میکن

امروز خوشم بدار و فردا با من

آنچه از کرمت سزد بما آن میکن

۳٦٥

آنرا که وقوفست بر احوالِ جهان

شادی و غم و رنج برُو شد یکسان

چون نیك و بدِ جهان بسر خواهد شد

خواهی تو بدرد باش و خواهی درمان

---

364. C. L. N. A. I. J. In line 4 scan *ánchaz*.

365. C. L. N. A. B. I. J. H. *Khwāhī tu bāsh,* " whether you be."

366.

Lament not fortune's mutability,
But up! and seize her favours ere they flee:
    If the world's course were ruled by constancy,
Luck would not others leave to come to thee.

367.

Best of old friends! give ear to what I say,
Let not heaven's treacherous wheel your heart
        dismay;
    But rest contented in your humble nook,
And watch the tricks that wheel is wont to
        play.

368.

Hear now Khayyám's advice, and bear in mind,
Consort with revellers, though they be maligned,
    Cast down the gates of abstinence and prayer,
Yea, drink, and even rob, so you be kind!

---

366. C. L. N. A. I. J. This was a saying of Kisra
Parviz to his Sultana.   Bicknell's Hafiz, p. 73.
    367. C. L. N. A. I. J.

۳٦٦

بر خیز و مخور غمِ جهانِ گذران
خوشباش و دمی بشادمانی گذران
در طبعِ جهان اگر وفائی بودی
نوبت بتو خود نیامدی از دگران

۳٦۷

بشنو ز من ای زبدهٔ یارانِ کهن
اندیشه مکن زین فلک بیسر و بن
در کوشهٔ عرصهٔ قناعت بنشین
بازیچهٔ چرخ را تماشا میکن

۳٦۸

تا بتوانی خدمتِ رندان میکن
بنیادِ نماز و روزه ویران میکن
بشنو سخنِ راست ز خیّام ای دوست
می میخور و ره میزن و احسان میکن

368. C. L. N. A. B. I. J. A rather violent extension of
he doctrine, Mercy is better than sacrifice.

369.

The world's a body and the "Truth" its soul.
The angels are its senses, they control
    Its limbs—the creatures, elements and spheres;
All *seem* to be, ONE only *is* the whole.

370.

Last night that idol who enchants my heart,
Longing to purify and cheer my heart,
    Gave me his cup to drink ; when I refused.
He said, " Drink then to gratify *my* heart

371.

Wouldst thou have fortune bow her neck to
        thee,
Make it thy care to feed thy soul with glee :
    And hold a creed like mine, which is, to drain
The cup of wine, not that of misery.

---

369. L N. Cp. Pope,
    "All are but parts of one stupendous whole.
    Whose body Nature is and God the soul. ' &c. ;
and M Pattison's note. Acts xvii. 28 , Virgil, Georgics,
iv 221 , Wordsworth, "Above Tintern, ' &c.

۳٦۹

حق جانِ جهانست و جهان جمله بدن
واصنافِ ملائكةِ حواسِ اين نن
افلاك و عناصر و مواليد اعضا
توحيد همين است و دگرها همه فن

۳۷۰

ديشب ز سرِ صدقِ و صفاي دلِ من
در ميكده آن روح فزايِ دل من
جامي بمن آورد كه بستان و بخور
گفتم نخورم گفت براي دلِ من

۳۷۱

خواهي بنهد پيشِ تو گردون گردن
كارِ تو بود هميشه جان پروردن
همچون منت اعتقاد بايد كردن
مي خوردن و اندوهِ جهان نا خوردن

---

370 N

371. L N. So the Ecclesiast "There is nothing better
for a man than that he should eat, and drink, and make
his soul enjoy good in his labour"

372.

Though you survey, O my enlightened friend,
This world of vanity from end to end,
   You will discover there no other good
Than wine and rosy cheeks, you may depend !

373.

Last night upon the river bank we lay,
I with my wine-cup, and a maiden gay,
   So bright it shone, like pearl within its shell.
The watchman cried, " Behold the break of
      day !"

374.

Have you no shame for all the ill you do,
Sins of omission and commission too ?
   Suppose you gain the world, you can but
      leave it,
You cannot carry it away with you !

---

372. N. Note *izáfat* dropped after *sáhib*. Bl., Prosody,
p 14

373. N. H. *Nigárè.* Here *ya* may be *yi i tankír*. the

۳۷۲

در عالمِ خاك از كران تا بكران

چندانكه نظر كنند صاحب نظران

حاصل ز جهانِ بيوفا چيزى نيست

اّلا مىِ لعل و عارضِ خوش پسران

۳۷۳

دى بر لبِ جوى با نگارى موزون

من بودم و ساغرِ شرابِ گلگون

در پيش نهاده صدفى كز گهرش

نوبت‌زنِ صبحِ صادق آيد بيرون

۳۷۴

شرمت نايد ازين تباهى كردن

زين تركِ اوامر و نواهى كردن

گيرم كه سراسر اينجيان ملكِ تو شد

جـز آن كه رها كنى چه خواهى كردن

---

izáfat being dispensed with (Lumsden, ii. 296), [?] or perhaps *ya i tausifi* before the " sifat " *mawzún.*

374. C. L. N. A. I. J.

375.

An outlaw in the desert did I see,
He had no wealth, no faith, no heresy,

   No God, no truth, no law, no certitude ;
In the two worlds where's man so bold as he ?

376.

Some look for truth in creeds, and forms, and
       rules ;
Some grope for doubts or dogmas in the schools :

   But from behind the veil a voice proclaims,
" Your road lies neither here nor there, O fools '

377.

In heaven is seen the bull we name Parwin,
Beneath the earth another lurks unseen :

   And thus to wisdom's eyes mankind appear
A drove of asses, these two bulls between !

---

375. L N. A *beshara'* or antinomian Sufi
376 C L N A 1. Truth, hidden from theologians
and philosophers, is revealed to mystics See *Gulshan i
Ráz*, p. 11 ; *Masnari*, p. 305.

٣٧٥

رندی دیدم نشسته بر خشك زمین
نه كفر و نه اسلام و نه دنیا و نه دین
نه حق نه حقیقت نه شریعت نه یقین
اندر دو جهان كرا بُوَد زهرهٔ این

٣٧٦

قومی متفكّرند در مذهب و دین
جمعی متحیّرند در شكّ و یقین
ناگاه منادئی بر آید ز كمین
كای بیخبران راه نه آنست و نه این

٣٧٧

گاویست در آسمان و نامش پروین
یك گاو دگر نهفته در زیرِ زمین
چشمِ خردت كشای چون اهلِ یقین
زیر و زبرِ دو گاو مشتی خر بین

---

377 L. N. The bulls are the constellation Taurus, and
that which supports the earth *Mushtí,* "a handful,"
izáfat displaced by *yá i tankír,* Lumsden, ii. 269.

378.

They say, " Endeavour to drink somewhat less ;
What reasons have you for such grave excess ? "
   " First, my love's face ; second, my morning
      wine.
Can any more lucidity possess ? "

379.

Had I the power great Allah to advise,
I'd bid him sweep away this earth and skies,
   And build a better world, where man might
      hope
His heart's desire perchance to realise.

380.

My heart weighed down by folly, grief and tine,
Is e'er inebriate with love divine ;
   Whenas the Loved One portioned out His
      wine,
With my heart's blood he filled this cup of mine !

---

378   C. L N A I J.

379   C L N. A I. J   This recalls the celebrated
speech of Alphonso X., king of Castile.

۳۷۸

گویند برایِ می که کمتر خور ازین
آخر بچه عذر بر نداری سر ازین
عذرم رخِ یار و بادهٔ صبحدمست
انصاف بده چه عذر روشنتر ازین

۳۷۹

گر بر فلکم دست بُدی چون یزدان
بر داشتمی من این فلکرا ز میان
از نو فلکِ دگر چنان ساختمی
کازاده بکامِ دل رسیدی آسان

۳۸۰

مسکین دلِ دردمندِ دیوانهٔ من
هشیار نشد ز عشقِ جانانهٔ من
روزی که شرابِ عاشقی میدادند
در خونِ جگر زدند پیمانهٔ من

---

380. C. L. N. A. I. Meaning, " the wine of life, or
existence, poured by the Deity into all beings at creation."
See *Gulshan i Ráz*, p. 80.

381.

To drain the cup, to hover round the fair,—
Can hypocritic arts with these compare ?
　　If all who love and drink are bound for hell,
There's many a wight of heaven may well
　　despair !

382.

Suffer not gloomy thoughts your joy to
　　drown,—
Nor let grief's millstone weigh your spirits down :
　　Since none can tell what is to be, 'tis best
With wine and love your heart's desires to
　　crown.

383.

Tis fine to be cried up and glorified,
Tis very mean at Heaven's duress to chide :
　　Still, head had better ache with over-drink,
Than be puffed up with pharisaic pride.

---

381. L. N. B Note the plural *nekuán* formed without
the euphonic *yá*. Scan *nekúwan* Comp. No. 67.

۳۸۱

میخوردن و گردِ نیکوان گردیدن

به زانکه بزرق و زاهدی ورزیدن

گر عاشق و مست دوزخی خواهد بود

پس رویِ بهشت کس نخواهد دیدن

۳۸۲

نتّوان دلِ شاد را بغم فرسودن

وقتِ خوشِ خود بسنگِ محنت سودن

در دهر که داند که چه خواهد بودن

می باید و معشوق و بکام آسودن

۳۸۳

نیکست بنامِ نیك مشهور شدن

عارست ز جورِ چرخ رنجور شدن

خمّار ببویِ آبِ انگور شدن

به زانکه بزهدِ خویش مغرور شدن

382. C. L. N. A. B. I. J.

383. C. L. N. A. I. J. Compare Tartufe, i. 6.

384.

Pity, O Lord, this prisoned heart, I pray,
Pity this bosom stricken with dismay!
  Pardon these hands that ever grasp the cup,
These feet that to the tavern ever stray!

385.

From self-reliance, Lord, deliver me,
Sever from self, and occupy with Thee!
  When sober I am bondman to the world,
Make me beside myself, and set me free!

386.

See what foul tricks this circling dome doth
        play!
See earth left empty of friends snatched away!
  To live the one breath you can call your own
Look for no morrow, mourn no yesterday!

---

384 N.
385 C L N A I J A mystic's prayer. L reads
wai̇zad, " he labours,' exertion (?) N reads zi̇ ṛah i bésh u
kamam. See Masnavi, p. 317 Note tashdíd on rabb dropped

۳۸۴

یا رب بدلِ اسیرِ من رحمت کن
بر سینهٔ غم پذیرِ من رحمت کن
بر پایِ خرابات رو من بخشای
بر دست پیاله گیرِ من رحمت کن

۳۸۵

یا رب ز قبولِ ورزدم باز رهان
مشغول خودت کن ز خودم باز رهان
تا هشیارم ز نیك و بد میدانم
مستم کن و از نیك و بدم باز رهان

۳۸۶

زین گنبد گردیده بد افعالی بین
وز رفتنِ دوستان جهان خالی بین
تا بتوانی تو یك نفس خود را باش
فردا منگر دی مطلب حالی بین

---

386. L. B. I follow L. in reading *gardída*, "turning
round." Line 3, "In order that you may live the one
breath belonging to yourself." For this use of *rá* see
Lumsden, ii., 517, Rule 6.

387.

Since all we gain in this abode of woe
Is sorrow's pangs to feel, and grief to know.
　　Happy are they that never come at all,
And they that, having come, the soonest go!

388.

By reason's dictates it is right to live,
But of ourselves we know not how to live,
　　So Fortune, like a master, rod in hand.
Raps our pates well to teach us how to live!

389.

Nor you nor I can read the etern decree,
To that enigma we can find no key;
　　They talk of you and me *behind* the veil.
But if the veil be lifted, where are *we?*

---

387 C L A B I J Compare the chorus in the
Oedipus Coloneus, " The best lot is never to be born
(line 1224, &c.).
388. L. Fortune's buffets.

۳۸۷

چون حاصلِ آدمی در این شورستان

جز خوردنِ غصّه نیست یا کندنِ جان

خرّم دلِ آن که زین جهان زود برفت

آسوده کسی که خود نیامد بجهان

۳۸۸

بر موجبِ عقل زندگانی کردن

شاید کردن ولی ندانی کردن

استادِ تو روزگار چابکدستست

چندان بسرت زند که دانی کردن

۳۸۹

اسرارِ ازل را نه تو دانی و نه من

وین حرفِ معمّا نه تو خوانی و نه من

هست از پسِ پرده گفتگوئی من و تو

چون پرده برافتد نه تو مانی و نه من

---

389. C. L. A. I. J. Meaning, we are part of the
"veil of phenomena," which hides the Divine Noumenon.
If that be swept away what becomes of us? See *Gulshan i
Ráz*, p. 63, note 1.

390.

These heavens, my Love, roll on with fixed
     design
To snatch away thy precious life, and mine;
  Sit we upon this turf, 'twill not be long
Ere turf shall grow upon my dust, and thine !

391.

When our souls from our bodies pass away.
These bodies 'neath a tomb of bricks they'll lay.
  And not long after, for another's tomb,
Other bricks will be moulded from our clay.

392.

Yon palace, towering to the welkin blue,
Where kings did bow them down, and homage
    do,—
  I saw a ringdove on its turrets perched,
And thus he made complaint, " Coo, Coo, Coo.
    Coo ! "

---

390.   L N B
391.   L N. A. I.

٣٩٠

این چرخِ فلك بهرِ هلاكِ من و تو
قصدی دارد بجانِ پاكِ من و تو
بر سبزه نشین بتا که بس دیر نماند
تا سبزه برون دمد ز خاكِ من و تو

٣٩١

از تن چو برفت جانِ پاكِ من و تو
خشتی دو نهند بر مغاكِ من و تو
وانگه ز برایِ خشتِ گورِ دگران
در کالبدی کشند خاكِ من و تو

٣٩٢

آن قصر که بر چرخ همی زد پهلو
بر درگهِ او شهان نهادندی رو
دیدیم که بر کنگرِ اش فاخته‌ء
آواز همیداد که کو کو کو کو

---

392. C. L. N. A. I. J. Binning found this quatrain
inscribed on the ruins of Persepolis. FitzGerald. Coo
(*Kú*) means " Where are they ? "

393.

We come and go, but for the gain, where is it?
And spin life's woof, but for the warp, where is
it?
　　And many a righteous man has burned to
　　dust
In heaven's blue rondure, but their smoke,
　　where is it?

394.

The fount of life is in that lip of thine.
Let not the cup's lip touch that lip of thine!
　　Beshrew me, if I fail to drink his blood,
For who is he, to touch that lip of thine?

395.

Such as I am, Thy power created me,
Thy care hath kept me for a century!
　　Through all these years I make experiment,
If *my* sins or *Thy* mercy greater be.

---

393. C L N A. B I J. So Ecclesiastes, "There is
no remembrance of the wise, more than of the fool"
"Smoke," *i.e* trace.

۳۹۳

از آمدن و رفتنِ ما سودی کو

وز تارِ وجودِ عمرِ ما پودی کو

در چنبرِ چرخ جسمِ چندین پاکان

میسوزد و خاك میشود دودی کو

۳۹٤

ای آبِ حیات مضمّر اندر لبِ تو

مگذار که بوسد لبِ ساغر لبِ تو

گر خونِ صراحی نخورم مردِ نیم

او خود که بود که لب نهد بر لبِ تو

۳۹٥

آنم که پدید گشتم از قدرتِ تو

صد ساله شدم بناز و نعمتِ تو

صد سال باِمتحان گنه خواهم کرد

یا جرمِ منست بیش یا رحمتِ تو

---

394. C. L. N. A. I. J. To a sweetheart.

395. C. L. N. A. I. J. God's long-suffering.

396.

" Take up thy cup and goblet, Love," I said,

" Haunt purling river-bank, and grassy glade ;

   Full many a moon-like form has heaven's
      wheel

Oft into cup, oft into goblet, made !"

397.

We buy new wine and old, our cups to fill,

And sell for two grains this world's good and
      ill ;

   Know you where you will go to after death ?

Set wine before me, and go where you will !

398.

Was e'er man born who never went astray ?

Did ever mortal pass a sinless day ?

   If I do ill and Thou requite with ill,

Wherein does our behaviour differ, pray ?

---

396. C L N. A. B. I J. B. reads *júy* and *sabúy* and
has other variants

٣٩٦

بر دار پیاله و سبو ای دلجو

بر گَرَدِ بگردِ سبزهٔزار و لبِ جو

کین چرخ بسی قدِّ بتانِ مهرو

صد بار پیاله کرد و صد بار سبو

٣٩٧

مائیم خریدارِ می کهنه و نو

وانگاه فروشندهٔ عالم بدو جو

دانی که پس از مرگ کجا خواهی رفت

می پیشِ من آر و هر کجا خواهی رو

٣٩٨

ذا کرده گناه در جهان کیست بگو

وانکس که گنه نکرد چون زیست بگو

من بد کنم و تو بد مکافات دهی

پس فرق میانِ من و تو چیست بگو

399.

Where is that ruby gem of Badakhshán,
That spirit's balm, that scented origan ?

　They say 'tis wrong for Musulmáns to drink,
But tell me where to find a Musulmán ?

400.

My body's life and strength proceed from Thee !
My soul within and spirit are of Thee !

　My being is of Thee, and Thou art mine,
And I am Thine, since I am lost in Thee !

401.

Man, like a ball, hither and thither goes,
As the strong bat of fate directs the blows :

　But He, who gave thee up to this rude sport,
He knows what drives thee, yea, He knows, He
　　knows !

---

399. C L N. A I J Some MSS read *labála l.*
Origan, marjoram. The pun on *ráhat* and *ráh* cannot be
reproduced

400. L Cp. Acts xvii. 28.

٣٩٩

یاقوتِ لبِ لعلِ بدخشانی کو
وان راحتِ روح و راح ریحانی کو
گویند حرام در مسلمانی شد
تو می خور و غم مخور مسلمانی کو

۴۰۰

ای زندگیِ تن و توانم همه تو
جانی و دلی ای دل و جانم همه تو
تو هستیِ من شدی ازانی همه من
من نیست شدم در تو ازانم همه تو

۴۰۱

ای رفته بچوگانِ قضا همچو گو
چپ می خورد و راست برو هیچ مگو
کانکس که ترا فگند اندر تک و پو
او داند او داند او داند او

---

401. C. L. A. I. J. Line 4 is in metre 22, consisting of
ten syllables, all long. The *alifs* after each *dánad* are treated
as ordinary consonants. Bl., Prosody, p. 10. So Virgil uses
spondees to give emphasis, in *Monstrum horrendum*, &c.

402.

O Thou who givest sight to emmet's eyes,
And strength to puny limbs of feeble flies,
  To Thee we will ascribe omnipotence,
No meaner attribute to Thee applies.

403.

Let not base avarice enslave thy mind,
Nor vain ambition in its trammels bind;
  Be sharp as fire, as running water swift,
Not, like earth's dust, the sport of every wind '

404.

'Tis best all else but gladness to forego,
And wine that charming Turki maids bestow;
  Kalandars' revels pass all things that are,
From moon on high down unto fish below '

---

402 L Perhaps alluding to the anthropomorphist
controversy at Nishapūr.
  403. L C A. I J
  404. C. L. N. A. B. I. J. For *mai* L reads *ha jj.*

۴۰۲

در دیدهٔ تنگِ مور نورست از تو
در پای ضعیفِ پشه زورست از تو
ذاتِ تو سزاست مر خداوندی را
هر وصف که ناسزاست دورست از تو

۴۰۳

گر باخردی تو حرص را بنده مشو
در پایِ طمع خوار و سرافکنده مشو
چون آتش تیز باش چون آب روان
چون خاک بهر باد پراکنده مشو

۴۰۴

از هر چه بجز مَی است کوتاهی به
می هم ز کفِ بتانِ خرگاهی به
مستیّ و قلندری و گمراهی به
یکجرعهٔ می ز ماه تا ماهی به

---

probably a Sufi gloss. In line 3 scan *mastiyy-ŏ*. Bl.,
Prosody, p. 11. Fish, that whereon the earth was said to
rest. *Kharyáh*, a Turkoman tent. Kalandars, antinomian
dervishes.

405.

Why trouble thus, O friend, about thy lot?
Let these vain cares be once for all forgot;

Thy garb of life will soon be torn to shreds,
And stains of word or deed will matter not.

406.

O thou who hast done ill, and ill alone,
And thinkest to find mercy at the Throne,

Hope not for mercy! for good left undone
Cannot be done, nor evil done undone!

407.

Count not to live beyond your sixtieth year:
To walk in jovial courses persevere:

And ere your skull be turned into a cup,
Let wine-cup ever to your hand adhere!

---

405. L N
406   N. A l.   This quatrain is by Abu Sa'id   (Ethé

۴۰۵

ای یار ز روزگار باش آسوده
واندوهِ زمانه کم خور از بیهوده
چون کسوتِ عمر بر تنت چاك شود
چه کرده و چه گفته و چه آلوده

۴۰۶

ای نیك نکرده و بدیها کرده
وانگاه بلطفِ حق توّلا کرده
بر عفو مکن تکیه که هرگز نبود
ناکرده چو کرده کرده چون ناکرده

۴۰۷

اندازهٴ عمر بیش از شصت منه
هر جا که قدم نهٴ بجز مست منه
زان پیش که کلّهٴ سرت کوزه کنند
رو کوزه ز دوش و کاسه از دست منه

No. 8. S.); and is an answer to No. 420, which is attributed
to Avicena.   407. L. N. B.

408.

These heavens resemble an inverted cup,
Whereto the wise in helplessness look up :
   So stoops the bottle o'er his love the glass,
Feigning to kiss, and gives her blood to sup !

409.

I sweep the tavern threshold with my hair,
The two worlds' good and ill cause me no care :
   Should those two balls roll to my door. when
      drunk,
For just one barleycorn I'd sell the pair !

410

The drop wept for his severance from the sea,
But the sea smiled, for, " I am all," said he :
   Yea, God is all in all, there's none beside,
But one point circling seems diversity.

—

408. C L N. A. B I Blood. an emblem of life
Cp No 229.

409 L N B Bar man ba juice. ' To me t would be
as a barleycorn "

۴۰۸

این چرخ چو طاسیست نگون افتاده

در وی همه زیرکان زبون افتاده

در دوستیِ شیشه و ساغر نگرید

لب بر لب و در میانه خون افتاده

۴۰۹

ای من در میخانه بسبلت رفته

ترکِ بد و نیکِ هر دو عالم گفته

گر هر دو جهان چو گوی افتد بکوی

بر من بجوی چو مست باشم خفته

۴۱۰

قطره بگریست که از بحر جدائیم همه

بحر بر قطره بخندید که مائیم همه

در حقیقت دگری نیست خدائیم همه

لیک از گردشِ یک نقطه جدائیم همه

<hr />

410. N. Ramal metre, No. 50.

"Whirl round one spark of fire,

And from its quick motion it appears a circle."

Gulshan i Ráz, l. 710. Cp. *Masnavi*, p. 24, and Tennyson

"Higher Pantheism."

411.

Shall I still sigh for what I have not got,
Or try with cheerfulness to bear my lot ?
  Fill up my cup ! I know not if the breath
I now am drawing is my last, or not !

412.

Yield not to grief, though fortune prove unkind.
Nor call sad thoughts of parted friends to mind :
  Devote thy heart to sugary lips, and wine,
Fling not thy precious life unto the wind !

413.

Of mosque and prayer and fast preach not to me.
Rather go drink, were it on charity !
  Yea, drink, Khayyám ! full soon they'll take
     thy dust
And jug, or cup, or pitcher, make of thee !

---

411   C L N A B. I J. Some MSS place this
quatrain under *Radif Ya*
  412   L N B

۴۱۱

تا کی غمِ آن خورم که دارم یا نه
وین عمر بخوشدلی گذارم یا نه
پر کن قدحِ باده که معلومم نیست
کین دم که فرو برم بر آرم یا نه

۴۱۲

تن در غمِ روزگارِ بیداد مده
جانرا ز غمِ گذشتگان یاد مده
دل جز بشکر لبِ پریزاد مده
بی باده مباش و عمر بر باد مده

۴۱۳

تا چند ز مسجد و نماز و روزه
در میکدها مست شو از دریوزه
خیّام بخور باده که این خاکِ ترا
گه جام کنند و گه سبو گه کوزه

---

413. N. "Imperial Cæsar, dead, and turned to clay,
        Might stop a hole to keep the wind away."

414.

Bulbuls, doting on roses, oft complain
How froward breezes rend their veils in twain ;
    Sit we beneath this rose, which many a time
Has sprung from earth, and dropped to earth
    again.

415.

Suppose the world goes well with you. what
    then ?
When life's last page is read and turned, what
    then ?
    Suppose you live a hundred years of bliss.
Yea, and a hundred more to boot, what then ?

416.

How is it that of all the leafy tribe,
Cypress and lily men as " free " describe ?
    This has a dozen tongues, yet holds her peace.
That has a hundred hands which take no bribe.

— —

414. L N B
415. C. L N A I J. *Rínda*, see Vullers, p 100

۴۱۴

بنگر ز صبا دامنِ گل چاک شده
بلبل ز جمالِ گل طربناک شده
در سایهٔ گل نشین که بسیار این گل
از خاک بر آمدست و بر خاک شده

۴۱۵

دنیا بمراد راننده گیر آخر چه
وین نامهٔ عمر خوانده گیر آخر چه
گیرم که بکامِ دل بمانی صد سال
صد سال دگر بمانده گیر آخر چه

۴۱۶

دانی ز چه روی اوفتادست و چه راه
آزادیِ سرو و سوسن اندر افواه
این دارد ده زبان ولیکن خاموش
وان دارد صد دست ولیکن کوتاه

---

416. L. N. Sa'di in the *Gulistan*, Book viii., gives
another explanation of this expression. " Tongues, stamens,
and hands, branches."

117.

Cupbearer! fetch delicious wine and hand it!
Produce that darling of my heart and hand it!
　That pleasing chain which tangles in its coils
Wise men and fools alike,—make haste to hand
　　it!

418.

Alas! my wasted life has gone to wrack!
What with forbidden meats, and drink, alack!
　And leaving undone what 'twas right to do,
And doing wrong, my face is very black!

419.

I could repent of all, but of wine, never!
I could dispense with all, but with wine, never!
　If I should come to be true Musulman,
Could I abjure my Magian wine? no, never!

---

117. L. N. *Bipéchand* seems a plural of dignity
418 C. L N A I *Harám*, the predicate of *lakma*.

۴۱۷

ساقی می خوشگوار بر دستم نه
وان بادهٔ چون نگار بر دستم نه
آن می که چو زنجیر بپیچند بهم
دیوانه و هوشیار بر دستم نه

۴۱۸

فریاد که رفت عمر بر بیهوده
هم لقمه حرام و هم نفس آلوده
فرمودهٔ نا کرده سیه رویم کرد
فریاد ز کردهای نا فرموده

۴۱۹

من توبه کنم از همه چیز از می نه
کز جمله گزیر باشدم از وی نه
امّا بود آنکه من مسلمان گردم
وین ترک می مغانه کویم هی نه

---

419. L. N. The Magians (Maghs) sold wine.

420.

Once in Thy mercy we've obtained a place,
The law's commands no longer rule our case:
    Ill done is undone, good undone is done,
Where'er extends the ambit of free grace.

421.

This is the form Thou gavest me of old,
Wherein Thou workest marvels manifold :
    Can I aspire to be a better man,
Or other than I issued from Thy mould ?

422.

O Lord! to Thee all creatures worship pay,
To Thee both small and great for ever pray :
    Thou takest woe away, and givest weal :
Give, then, and in Thy mercy take away !

420   L. N. A. 1   Ascribed to Avicena   (Ethé No 1)
Compare Romans viii 2.   Tawalla, " obtaining a situation "
" being chosen as a friend "
421   C. L. N A. I.   This is a variation of No. 221

۴۲۰

مائیم بلطفِ تو توکّل کرده

وز طاعت و معصیت تبرّا کرده

آنجا که عنایتِ تو باشد باشد

ناکرده چو کرده کرده چون ناکرده

۴۲۱

نقشیست که بر وجودِ ما ریخته‌ء

صد بوالعجبی ز ما بر انگیخته‌ء

من زان به ازین نمیتوانم بودن

کز بوته مرا چنین فرو ریخته‌ء

۴۲۲

ای در رهِ بندگیت یکسان که و مه

در هر دو جهان خدمتِ درگاهِ تو به

نکبت تو ستانّی و سعادت تو دهی

یا رب تو بفضلِ خویش بستان و بده

---

422. L. Scan *bandayita*, omitting *fatha* before *te*.
Vullers, p. 197. Also ascribed to Abu Sa'id. (Ethé
No. 45.) S. T.

423.

Thou wentest and returnest as a quadruped,
Thy name from human memories has fled,
    Thy nails have grown and thickened into
        hoofs,
Thou 'st shed thy beard and grown a tail instead.

424.

O unenlightened race of humankind,
Ye are a nothing, built on empty wind !
    Yea, a mere nothing, hovering in the abyss,
A void before you, and a void behind !

425.

Each morn I vow, " To-night I will repent
Of wine, and tavern haunts no more frequent ;"
    But now 'tis spring, so loose me from my
        vow,
While roses blossom, how can I repent ?

---

423   C. L A I. J   Impromtu on an ass, in whom
Omar affected to recognize the spirit of a late Molla   See
R. A S. Journal, vol xxx. p 359.   In line 1 some MSS

۴۲۳

اى رفته و باز آمده و خم گشته

نامت ز میانِ مردمان گم گشته

ناخن همه جمع آمده و سُم گشته

ریش از پسِ کون آمده و دُم گشته

۴۲۴

اى بیخبر از کارِ جهان هیچ نهٔ

بنیاد بباد ست ازان هیچ نهٔ

شد حدِّ وجود در میانِ دو عدم

اطراف بود تو در میان هیچ نهٔ

۴۲۵

هر روز برانم که کنم شب توبه

از جام و پیالهٔ لبالب توبه

اکنون که رسید وقتِ گل ترکم ده

در موسمِ گل ز توبه یا رب توبه

---

read *ham*; Mr. Beveridge found *kham* in five MSS. of the
Tarikh i Alfi.

424. C. L. A. I. J. Cp. *Gulistan*, viii. 33.

425. C. L. A. I. J. *Tauba*, repentance, also breaking vows.

426.

Vain study of philosophy eschew!
Rather let tangled curls attract your view :
   And shed the bottle's life-blood in your cup,
Or e'er death shed your blood, and feast on you

427.

O heart! that riddle thou wilt never read,
That point on which the wise are not agreed :
   Quaff wine, and make thy heaven here below,
Who knows if heaven above will be thy meed ?

428.

They that have passed away, and gone before,
Sleep in delusion's dust for evermore :
   Go, boy, and fetch some wine, this is the
      truth,
Their dogmas were but air, and wind their lore !

---

426   C. L. N A B I. J. *Bygurčzi bi*, "better that
you should eschew."
   427.   C L. N A. B I J.

۴۲٦

از درسِ علومِ جمله بگریزی به
واندر سرِ زلفِ دلبر آویزی به
زان پیس که روزگار خونت ریزد
تو خونِ صراحی بقدح ریزی به

۴۲۷

ای دل تو باسرارِ معمّا نرسی
در نکتهٴ زیرکانِ دانا نرسی
اینجا بمی و جامِ بهشتی میساز
کانجا که بهشتست رسی یا نرسی

۴۲۸

آنان که ز پیش رفته اند ای ساقی
در خاكِ غرور خفته اند ای ساقی
رو باده خور و حقیقت از من بشنو
بادست هر آنچه گفته اند ای ساقی

428. C. L. N. A. B. I. J. So Ecclesiastes, "I gave my
heart to know wisdom . . . . and perceived that this also is
vanity."

429.

O heart! when on the Loved One's sweets you
    feed,
You lose youself, yet find your Self indeed ;
    And, when you drink of His entrancing cup.
You hasten your escape from quick and dead !

430.

I take it hard that men should rail at me,
Whene'er I swerve from strict sobriety ;
    Ah ! if all peccadilloes made us drunk,
How many sober persons should I see ?

431.

Child of four elements and sevenfold heaven.
Who fume and sweat because of these eleven.
    Drink ! I have told you seventy times and
        seven,
Once gone. nor hell will send you back. nor
    heaven.

---

429   C L N A. 1 J   Die to self, to live in God. your
true self. See Max Muller, Hibbert Lectures, p 375
    430.   C. N. A. I. J

۴۲۹

ای دل چو ببزم ِ آن صنم بنشستی

از خویش بریدّی و بخود پیوستی

از جامِ فنا چو جرعءِ نوشیدی

از بود و نبودگان بکلّی رستی

۴۳۰

افتاد مرا با می و مستی کاری

خلقم بچه میکنند ملامت باری

ای کاش که هر حرام مستی کردی

تا من بجهان ندیدمی هشیاری

۴۳۱

ای آنکه نتیجهءِ چهار و هفتی

در هفت و چهار دائم اندر تفتی

می خور که چهار بار بیشت گفتم

باز آمدنت نیست چو رفتی رفتی

---

431. C. L. N. A. I. J. *I.e.* the four elements and the
seven spheres, called the "fourfold mothers" and the
"sevenfold fathers." Palmer, Oriental Mysticism. p. 32.

432.

With many a snare Thou dost beset my way,
And threatenest, if I fall therein, to slay ;

Thy laws pervade the universe, yet Thou
Imputest sin, when I do but obey !

433.

To Thee, whose essence baffles human thought,
Our sins and righteousness alike seem nought ;

May Thy grace sober me, though drunk with
sin,
And pardon all the ill that I have wrought !

434.

Could our life here proceed in blind routine,
Each single day a holiday had been :

Each man might satisfy his heart's desire,
Did no vain prohibitions intervene.

---

432   B N. God is the one real agent, *Fa'il i haqiqi.*
In l 4, I read *hukme* for *hukm i*

433   L N. Man cannot conceive the Absolute   So
Dean Mansel and H Spencer

۴۳۲

بر رهگذرم هزار جا دام نهی
گوئی کُشمت اگر در او گام نهی
یك ذرّه ز حکمِ تو جهان خالی نیست
حکمی تو کنی و عاصیم نام نهی

۴۳۳

ای از حرمِ ذاتِ تو عقل آگه نی
وز معصیت و طاعت ما مستغنی
مستم ز گناه و از رجا هشیارم
اُمید برحمتِ تو دارم یعنی

۴۳۴

این کارِ جهان اگر بتقلیدستی
هر روز بجایِ خویشتن عیدستی
هر کس بمرادِ خویش دستی بزدی
گر زانکه نه این بیهُده تهدیدستی

---

434. N. *Taqlíd*, following authority blindly. *Gulshan i Ráz*, p. 11, note 5. *I.e.* the authority of natural law " the law in the members." Prohibitions, *i.e.* " Touch not, taste not, etc." Col. ii. 21.

435.

O wheel of heaven, you thwart my heart's
      desire,
And rend to shreds my jubilant attire,
  The water that I drink you foul with earth,
And turn the very air I breathe to fire!

436.

O soul! could you but doff this flesh and bone,
You'd soar a sprite about the heavenly throne;
  Had you no shame to leave that highest
      sphere,
And dwell an alien on this earthly zone?

437.

Ah, potter, stay thine hand! with ruthless art
Put not to such base use man's mortal part!
  See, thou art mangling on thy cruel wheel
Farídun's fingers, and Kai Khosrau's heart!

---

435 C. L. N. A I
436 C. L. N B A L

۴۳۵

ای چرخ دلم همیشه غمناک کنی

پیراهنِ خرّمیِ من چاک کنی

بادی که رسد بمن تو اش آب کنی

آبی که خورم تو در دهن خاک کنی

۴۳۶

ای دل ز غبارِ جسم اگر پاک شوی

تو روحِ مجرّدی بر افلاک شوی

عرش است نشیمنِ تو شرمت بادا

کائی و مقیمِ خطّهٔ خاک شوی

۴۳۷

ای کوزه‌گرا بکوش اگر هشیاری

تا چند کنی بر گلِ آدم خواری

انگشتِ فریدون و کفِ کیخسرو

بر چرخ نهادهٔ چه می پنداری

---

437. C. L. N. A. I. Farídun and Kai Khosrau were
ancient kings of Persia. Kai Khosrau is usually identified
with Cyrus.

438

Rose! thou art like the face of some sweet belle,
Wine! thou art like a pearl within its shell:
 But, Fortune, thou dost ever show thyself
A stranger, though I ought to know thee well!

439.

From this world's kitchen crave not to obtain
That food sometimes substantial, sometimes vain.
 Which greedy worldlings gorge to their own
  loss;
Renounce that loss, so loss shall prove thy gain!

440.

Grieve not the people's hearts with proud despite,
So that they cry to God the livelong night:
 Nor plume thee on thy wealth and handsome
  looks,
One may be marred, one stol'n this very night.

---

438 N *Mímáni*, You resemble.
439 L N. B (first two lines). *Dúd*, smoke, insubstantial food Line 2 lit., "How long eat you these real
and unreal cares?"

۴۳۸

ای گل تو بروی دلربا میمانی
وی مل تو بلعل جانفزا میمانی
ای بخت ستیزه کار هر دم با من
بیگانه‌تری و آشنا میمانی

۴۳۹

از مطبخِ دنیا تو همه دود خوری
تا چند غمانِ بود و نابود خوری
دنیا که بر اهلِ او زیانیست عظیم
گر ترکِ زیان کنی همه سود خوری

۴۴۰

ازارِ دلِ خلقِ مجوئیم شبی
تا بر نکشند یا رب ذیم شبی
بر مال و جمالِ خویشتن تکیه مکن
کانرا بشبی برند و اینرا بشبی

---

440 N. *Tá bai nakashand,* "Let us abstain from
oppressing people, so that they may not heave a sigh,
saying, O Lord." Perhaps addressed to some tyrannical
Amir

411.

Since at the first Thou madest me Thy bride,
What led Thee to divorce me from Thy side?

   Thou didst not mean to cast me off at first,
Then why now doom me in the world to abide?

442.

Ah! would there were a place of rest from pain,
Which we, poor pilgrims, might at last attain.

   And after many thousand wintry years,
Renew our life, like flowers, and bloom again!

443.

When in love's book I sought an augury,
Forth came these words of one in ecstasy,

   " Thrice happy he that hath a moon-like bride,
And long as years may his sweet moments be!"

---

441. L N Pre-existence of the soul in God. See
Masnari, p. 25 *Manat*, the affixed *te* (for *tnrā*) pertains
to the verb *namūd*, "pleased thee" Bl., Prosody,
p. xiii.

۴۴۱

اوّل بخودم چو آشنا میکردی
آخر ز خودم چرا جدا میکردی
چون ترکِ منّت نبود از روزِ نخست
سرگشته بعالمم چرا میکردی

۴۴۲

ای کاش که جایِ آرمیدن بودی
یا این رہ را بسر رسیدن بودی
کاش از پیِ صد هزار سال از دلِ خاك
چون سبزہ امیدِ نو دمیدن بودی

۴۴۳

از دفترِ عشق میکشودم فالی
ناگاہ ز سوز سینه صاحب حالی
میگفت خوشا کسی که در خانهٔ او
یاریست چو ماهّی و شبی چون سالی

---

442. C. N. A. I. J. In line 2, for *basar* some MSS.
read *rawe* and some *rahe.*

443. C. L. N. A. I. Compare the " *sortes Virgilianæ.*"
In line 4, scan *máhíyyá.* Bl., Prosody, p. 11.

444.

Winter is past, and spring-tide has begun,
Soon will the pages of life's book be done !
   Well saith the sage, " Life is a poison rank,
And antidote, save grape-juice, there is none."

445.

Dear soul ! if thou true Moslem elder be,
Drop saintly show and budge austerity,
   And quaff the wine that Murtaza purveys,
And toy with Houris for the time to be !

446.

Last night I dashed my cup against a stone,
In a mad drunken freak, as I must own ;
   And lo ! the cup cried out in agony,
" You too, like me, shall soon be overthrown."

---

444 C. L N A I. J

445. N   Note the change from the imperative to the
aorist In line 4 scan *Murtázísha*. Murtaza (Ali) is the

۴۴۴

از آمدنِ بهار و از رفتنِ دی
اوراقِ وجودِ ما همیگردد طی
می خور مخور اندوه که گفتست حکیم
غمهایِ جهان چو زهر و تریاکش می

۴۴۵

ای دل می و معشوق بکن در باقی
سالوس رها کن و مکن زرّاقی
گر پیر و احمدی خوری جامِ شراب
زان حوض که مرتضاش باشد ساقی

۴۴۶

بر سنگی زدم دوش سبوئی کاشی
سر مست بُدم که کردم این اوباشی
با من بزبانِ حال میگفت سبو
من چون تو بدم تو نیز چون من باشی

celestial cupbearer. "Budge doctors of the Stoic fur,"
Milton, *i.e.* surly.

446. C. L. N. A. B. I. *Sabóyiy, yá i batni,* joined to
the noun by euphonic or conjunctive *yí.*

447.

My heart is weary of hypocrisy,
Cupbearer, bring some wine, I beg of thee!
   This hooded cowl and prayer-mat pawn for
      wine,
Thus on a solid base I'll stablish me.

448.

Audit yourself, your true account to frame,
See! you go empty, as you empty came :
   You say, "I will not drink and peril life,"
But, drink or no, you *must* die all the same!

449.

Open the door! O Warder best and purest,
And guide the way, O Thou of guides the surest!
   Directors born of men shall not direct me,
Their counsel comes to naught, but Thou
     endurest!

---

447   N   *Bu* for *buwad*, " it may be."
448.   C. L. N. A I.   In line 2, scan *árwadīyŏ*.
449   C. L   N   A I. J.   In line 4 scan *fániyand*,

۴۴۷

بگرفت مرا ملالت از زرّاقی
بر خیز و سبک باده بیار ای ساقی
سجّاده و طیلسان بمی ساز گرو
تا بو که شود لافِ من اندر باقی

۴۴۸

بر گیر ز خود حساب اگر با خبری
کاوّل تو چه آوردی و آخر چه بری
گوئی نخورم باده که میباید مرد
میباید مرد اگر خوری یا نخوری

۴۴۹

بگشای درم که در گشاینده توئی
بنمای رهم که ره نماینده توئی
من دست بهیچ دستگیری ندهم
کایشان همه فانی اند و پاینده توئی

---

dissolving the long *yá*. "Opener" (*Fatḥah*), "Guide"
(*Hádi*), and "Director" (*Rashíd*) are among the ninety-
nine special names of God used in ejaculations (*Zikr*).

450.

In spiteful calumny you still persist,
Calling me "infidel" and "atheist";
   My faults I'll not deny, but prithee say
If foul abuse becomes a moralist?

451.

To gain a remedy, put up with pain,
Endure the anguish, healing to attain ;
   Though poor, be ever of a thankful mind,
'Tis the sure mode true riches to obtain.

452.

Give me a skin of wine, a crust of bread,
A pittance bare, a book of verse to read :
   With thee, O love, to share my solitude,
I would not take the Sultan's realm instead '

---

450   C. L. N A. I   In line 1, scan *qōyi-yoz*, Bl ,
Prosody, p 10   The *tashdid* of *munkir* is dropped
  451   L N   *Dáráyiy*   The first *ya* is the conjunctive
ya (Vullers, p 16), the second, *yá i tankir.*

۴۵۰

با من تو هر آنچه گوئی از کین گوئی
پیوسته مرا ملحد و بیدین گوئی
من خود مقرم بر آنچه هستم لیکن
انصاف بده ترا رسد کین گوئی

۴۵۱

با درد بساز تا دوائی یابی
وز رنج مذال تا شفائی یابی
میباش بوقت بیذوائی شاکر
تا عاقبت الامر نوائی یابی

۴۵۲

تنگی می لعل خواهم و دیوانی
سدِّ رمقی باید و نصفِ نانی
وانگه من و تو نشسته در ویرانی
خوشتر بود از مملکتِ سلطانی

---

452. N B *Tangé izáfat* displaced by *yá i tankir*,
Lumsden, ii 269 *Sadd i ramaqi*, "preventing the breath
from giving out," 'what keeps body and soul together."

453.

Reason not of the five, nor of the four,
Be their enigmas one, or many score.
  We are but earth ; go, minstrel, bring the
      lute :
We are but air ; bring wine, I ask no more!

454.

Why argue on Yá Sín and on Barát ?
Write me the draft for wine they call Barát !
  The day on which that draft shall honoured be,
Will seem to me as the great night Barát !

455.

Whilst thou dost wear this fleshly livery,
Step not beyond the bounds of destiny ;
  Bear up, though very Rustams be thy foes,
And take no favours e'en from Hatim Tai !

---

453 N C. L. A I J give only the first line of this
Five senses, four elements
  454. C L N. A I. J. *Ya Sin* is the 64th, and *Barat* the

۴۵۳

تا چند حدیثِ پنج و چار ای ساقی
مشکل چه یکی چه صد هزار ای ساقی
خاکیم همه چنگ بساز ای ساقی
بادیم همه باده بیار ای ساقی

۴۵۴

تا چند ز یاسین و برات ای ساقی
بنویس بمیخانه برات ای ساقی
روزی که برات ما بمیخانه برند
آنروز بود شبِ برات ای ساقی

۴۵۵

تا در تنِ تست استخوان و رگ و پی
از خانهٔ تقدیر منه بیرون پی
گردن منه ار خصم بود رستمِ زال
منّت مکش ار دوست بود حاتم طی

9th, chapter of the Koran. *Barát*, the "night of power."
455. C. L. N. A. I. J. Hatim Tai was famed for his
liberality.

156.

These ruby lips, and wine, and minstrel boys,
And lute, and pipe, your dearly cherished toys.
    Are mere redundancies, and you are naught,
Till you renounce the world's delusive joys.

457.

Bow down, heaven's tyranny to undergo,
Quaff wine to face the world and all its woe :
    Your origin and end are both in earth,
But now you are above ground, not below.

158.

You know the secret of this life, my dear !
Then why remain a prey to useless fear?
    Bend things to suit your whims you cannot ;
        yet
Cheer up for the few moments you are here !

----

156   L N *Hashw,* mere "stuffing," "leather or prunello."

۴۵۶

تا در هوسِ لعلِ لب و جامِ مئی
تا در پیِ آوازِ دف و چنگ و نئی
اینها همه حشو است خدا میداند
تا ترکِ تعلّق نکنی هیچ نئی

۴۵۷

تن زن چو بزیرِ فلک بیباکی
می نوش چو در عالمِ آفتناکی
چون اوّل و آخرت بجز خاکی نیست
انگار که در خاک نئی بر خاکی

۴۵۸

چون واقفی ای پسر ز هر اسراری
چندین چه خوری به بیهده تیماری
چون می نرود باختیاری کاری
حوش باش درین نفس که هستی باری

---

457. C. L. N. A. I. J. *Tan zadan*, to be patient.
458 C. L. N. A. I. J. Scan *chūn wāḳifunu*.

459.

Behold, where'er we turn our ravished eyes,
Sweet verdure springs, and crystal Kausar rise :
    And plains, once bare as hell, now smile as
        heaven :
Rest in this heaven with maids of Paradise !

460.

Never in this false world on friends rely,
(I give this counsel confidentially ;)
    Put up with pain, and seek no antidote
Endure your grief, and ask no sympathy !

461.

Of wisdom's precepts two are capital,
Outweighing all traditions doctrinal .
    " Better to fast than eat of every meat,
Better to live alone than mate with all ! "

---

459   C. L N A B I J   For *zĭ dĭzakh gūyĭ* (2n l
pers sing. aorist). B reads *zĭ dŏzakh gum gūy* (imperative)
but to make sense *zĭ* must then be altered to *ĭc ĭ*, " *And say*
hell is vanished "

۴۵۹

چندانکه نگاه میکنم هر سوئی
از سبزه بهشتست و ز کوثر جوئی
صحرا چو بهشت شد ز دوزخ گوئی
بنشین ببهشت با بهشتی روئی

۴۶۰

در شعبده خانهء جهان یار مجوی
بشنو ز من این حدیث و زنهار مگوی
با درد بساز و هیچ درمان مطلب
با غم بنشین خرّم و غمخوار مجوی

۴۶۱

دو چیز که هست مایهء دانائی
بهتر ز همه حدیث نا گویائی
از خوردنِ هر چه هست نا خوردن بِه
وز صحبتِ هر چه هست به تنهائی

---

460. N.

461. N. *Hadís i ná góyáyi.* The unwritten revelations,
or traditions, opposed to *Qur'án* (Koran), the "reading."
So *sruti* is opposed to *smriti.*

462.

Why unripe grapes are sharp, prithee explain,

And then grow sweet, while wine is sharp again

When one has carved a block into a lute,

Can he from that same block a flute obtain ?

463.

When dawn doth silver the dark firmament,

Why shrills the bird of dawning his lament ?

It is to show in dawn's bright looking-glass

How of thy careless life a night is spent.

464

Cupbearer, come ! from thy full-throated ewer

Pour blood-red wine, the world's despite to cure !

Where can I find another friend like wine,

So genuine, so solacing, so pure ?

---

462. L. N

463   C L N. A I J   So Job, " Hast spread the sky

۴٦۲

در باغ چو بدُ غوره ترش اوّلِ دی

شیرین ز چه گشت و تلخ چون آمد ی

از چوب بتیشه گرکسی کرد رباب

رز تیشه چگوئی تو که میسازد نی

۴٦۳

دانی که سپیده دم خروسِ سحری

هر لحظه چرا همیکند نوحه گری

یعنی که نمودند در آئینهٔ صبح

کز عمر شبی گذشت و تو بیخبری

۴٦۴

در ده می لعلِ لاله گونِ صافی

بکُشای ز حلقِ شیشه خونِ صافی

کامروز برون ز جامِ می نیست مرا

یکدوست که دارد اندرونِ صافی

465.

Though you should sit in sage Aristo's room,
Or rival Cæsar on his throne of Rúm,

 Drain Jamshed's goblet, for your end's the
  tomb,
Yea, were you Bahram's self, your end's the
  tomb !

466.

It chanced into a potter's shop I strayed,
He turned his wheel and deftly plied his trade,

 And out of monarchs' heads and beggars' feet
Covers and handles for his pitchers made !

467.

If you have sense, true senselessness attain,
And the Etern Cupbearer's goblet drain ;

 If not, true senselessness is not for you,
Not every fool true senselessness can gain !

---

465 N. *Jamhúr*, a name of Buzurjimihr, *Wazir* of
Núshirwán. *Faghfúr*, the Chinese emperor In line 1
scan *Aristúwú*, dissolving the long *u*
 466. C N L. A. I. J. *Páya*, "the treadle"

۴۶۵

در حکمت اگر ارسطو و جمهوری

در قدرت اگرچه قیصر و فغفوری

می نوش ز جام جم که گور آخر کار

گر بهرامی که عاقبت در گوری

۴۶۶

در کارگه کوزه‌گری کردم رای

در پایهٔ چرخ دیدم استاد بپای

میکرد دلیر کوزه را دسته و سر

از کلهٔ پادشاه و از پای گدای

۴۶۷

رو بیخبری گزین اگر باخبری

تا از کف مستان ازل باده خوری

تو بیخبری بیخبری کار تو نیست

هر بیخبری را نرسد بیخبری

---

467. L. N. Senselessness, *i.e.* the abnegation of carnal
knowledge for spiritual illumination. See *Gulshan i Ráz*,
p. 13, note 3.

468.

O Love ! before we pass death's portal through,
And potters make their jugs of me and you,
    Pour from this jug some wine, of headache
       void,
And fill your cup, and fill my goblet too '

469.

O Love ! while yet you can, with tender art,
Lift sorrow's burden from your lover's heart ;
    Others have lost their empery of charms,
And you erelong with yours will have to part.

470.

Bestir thee, ere death's cup for thee shall flow,
And blows of ruthless fortune lay thee low ;
    Acquire some substance *here*, for none is *there*
For those who empty-handed thither go '

---

468   C. L N A. I. J. Of headache void, in allusion to
the wine of Paradise, Koran, lvi 17.
  469. C. L. N. A. I J. Some MSS. read *zinhir* for

۴۶۸

زان بیشتر ای صنم که در رهگذری
خاكِ من و تو کوزه کند کوزه‌گری
زان کوزهء می که نیست در وی ضرری
پر کن قدحی بخور بمن ده دگری

۴۶۹

زنهار کنون که میتوانی باری
بر دار ز خاطرِ عزیزی باری
کین مملکتِ حسن نماند جاوید
از دستِ تو هَم برون رود یکباری

۴۷۰

زان پیش که از جامِ اجل مست شوی
زیرِ لگدِ حادثها پست شوی
سرمایه بدست آر اینجا کانجا
سودی نکنی اگر تهی دست شوی

---

zinhár. Either will scan.

470. L. N. Line 2 is in metre 4. Meaning, " Work
while it is day." See Ecclesiastes ix. 10.

471.

Who framed the lots of quick and dead but
    Thou ?
Who turns the troublous wheel of heaven but
    Thou ?
  Though we are sinful slaves, is it for Thee
To blame us ?   Who created us but Thou ?

472.

O wine, most limpid, pure, and crystalline,
Would I could drench with thee this frame of
    mine,
  So that the passers-by might think 'twas thou,
And cry, "Whence comest thou, good master
    wine ?"

473.

A Shaikh beheld a harlot, and quoth he,
" You seem a slave to drink and lechery ; "
  And she made answer, " What I seem I am.
But, Master, are *you* all you seem to be ? "

---

471. L N A I.   472. L N
173. L. N. The technical name of quatrains like this

۴۷۱

سازندهٔ کارِ مرده و زنده توئی

دارندهٔ این چرخِ پراگنده توئی

من گرچه بدم خواجهٔ این بنده توئی

کسرا چه گنه نه آفریننده توئی

۴۷۲

ای بادهٔ ناب و ای مِی مینائی

چندان بخورم ترا منِ شیدائی

کز دور مرا هر که به بیند گوید

ای خواجه شراب از کجا میائی

۴۷۳

شیخی بزنِ فاحشه گفتا مستی

هر لحظه بدامِ دیگری پابستی

گفتا شیخا هر آنچه گوئی هستم

امّا تو چنانکه مینمائی هستی

…rál o jawáb, or murája'at. Gladwin, Persian Rhetoric,
40

474.

If, like a ball, earth to my house were borne,
When drunk, I'd rate it at a barleycorn;

    Last night they offered me in pawn for wine,
But the rude vintner laughed that pledge to
      scorn.

475.

Now in thick clouds Thy face Thou dost im-
    merse,
And now display it in this universe;

    Thou the spectator, Thou the spectacle,
Sole to Thyself Thy glories dost rehearse.

476.

Better to make one soul rejoice with glee,
Than plant a desert with a colony;

    Rather one freeman bind with chains of love,
Than set a thousand prisoned captives free!

---

474.   C L N. A I J   Note the *yá i tankir* in *huyí*,
juyí, and *giruyí*   Cp No 409

475.   C. L N A I J   Cp Sa'dí, *Gulistan* ii 9
" The visions of the holy are now manifested, now with-

٤٧٤

عالم همه کر چو گوی افتد بکوئی

من مست و خراب خفته بر من بجوئی

دوشم بخرابات گرو میکردند

خمّار همیگفت که نیکو گروئی

٤٧٥

که گشته نهان رو بکسی ننمائی

که در صورِ کون و مکان پیدائی

این جلوهگری بخویشتن بنمائی

خود عینِ عیانّ و خودی بینائی

٤٧٦

گر رویِ زمین بجمله آباد کنی

چندان نبود که خاطری شاد کنی

گر بنده کنی بلطف آزادیرا

بهتر که هزار بنده آزاد کنی

---

drawn;" Proverbs viii. 31, Vulgate version, "*ludens in orbe terrarum*," and *Gulshan i Ráz*, l. 775. Also Abu Sa'íd (Ethé, No. 17).

476. L. N. Cp Abu Sa'íd (Ethé, No. 1).

477.

O thou who for thy pleasure dost impart
A pang of sorrow to thy fellow's heart,
    Go! mourn thy perished wit, and peace of
        mind,
Thyself hast slain them, like the fool thou art!

478.

Wherever you can get two maunds of wine,
Set to, and drink it like a libertine;
    Whoso acts thus will set his spirit free
From saintly airs like yours, and grief like
    mine.

479.

So long as I possess two maunds of wine,
Bread of the flower of wheat, and mutton chine,
    And you, O Tulip-cheeks, to share my cell,
Not every Sultan's lot can vie with mine

---

477. C L N. A I J
478 C L. N. A B I J   *Chu man'*, "of one like me"
So in No 170, Vullers, p 254   Literally, "mustaches and

۴۷۷

گر شادیِ خویشتن بدان میدانی
کاسوده دلی را بغمی بنُشانی
در ماتمِ عقلِ خویش باشی همه عمر
میدار مصیبت که عجب نادانی

۴۷۸

گر زانکه بدست آید از می دو منی
می خور تو بهرِ محفل و هر انجمنی
کانکس که چنان کرد فراغت دارد
از سبلتِ چون توئی و ریشِ چو منی

۴۷۹

گر دست دهد ز مغزِ گندم نانی
وز می دو منی ز گوسفندی رانی
با لاله رخی نشسته در ویرانی
عیشی بود این نه حدِّ هر سلطانی

beard."

479. C. L. N. A. B. I. A variation of No. 452.

480.

They call you braggart if you 're widely known,
And deep dissembler if you live alone;

 Trust me, though you were Khizr or Elias,
'Twere best to know none and of none be known.

481.

Yes! here am I at my old tricks again,
I vowed repentance, but my vows were vain;

 Preach not to me about what Noah did,
But with a flood of wine my heart sustain!

482.

For union with my Love I sigh in vain,
The pangs of absence I can scarce sustain,

 My grief I dare not tell to any friend;
O trouble strange, sweet passion, bitter pain!

---

480 C. N I. So Sa'di, *Gulistán*, ii. 5 " Safety is in solitude "

481. C. L N. A. I. J. " Repentance of Nasuh," *i e*

۴۸۰

گر شهره شوی بشهر شرّ النّاسی
گر گوشه نشین شوی همه وسواسی
به زان نبود گر خضر و الیاسی
کس نشّناسد ترا تو کس نشّناسی

۴۸۱

ما و می و معشوق و صبوح ای ساقی
از ما نبود توبه نصوح ای ساقی
تا کی خوانی قصّهء نوح ای ساقی
پیش آر سبك راحتِ روح ای ساقی

۴۸۲

نه سویِ وصالِ تو مرا دست رسی
نه طاقتِ هجرانِ تو دارم نفسی
نه زهره که باز گویم این غم بکسی
مشکل کاری طُرفه غمی خوش هوسی

sincere. For his story see *Masnavi*, p. 249. In line 2, note *izáfat* dropped after silent *he*.

482. N. These quatrains are called *firákíya*, and are rare in Khayyám.

483.

'Tis morning, and I hear the call to prayer,
But budge I will not from my tavern-lair;
 Cupbearer, keep thy counsel to thyself !
Is this a time for preaching and for prayer ?

484.

Angel of joyful foot ! the dawn is nigh ;
Pour wine, and lift thy tuneful voice on high,
 Sing how Jamsheds and Khosraus bit the
  dust,
Whelmed by the rolling months from Tir to
 Dai !

485.

Frown not at revellers, I beg of thee,
For all thou keepest righteous company :
 But drink, for, drink or no, 'tis all the same,
If doomed to hell, no heaven thou'lt ever see.

---

483. C L N. A I J.
484. C L N A I. *Tir* and *Dai*, April and December.

۴۸۳

هنگامِ صبوح است و خروش ای ساقی

ما و می و کویِ میفروش ای ساقی

چه جایِ صلاحست خموش ای ساقی

بگذر ز حدیث و زهد نوش ای ساقی

۴۸۴

هنگامِ صبوح ای صنمِ فرّخ پی

بر ساز ترانه‌ء و پیش آور می

کافگند بخاك صد هزاران جم و کی

این آمدنِ تیر مه و رفتنِ دی

۴۸۵

هان تا بر مستان بدرشتی نشوی

یا از درِ نیکوان بزشتی نشوی

می خور که بخوردن و بناخوردنِ می

گر آلتِ دوزخی بهشتی نشوی

485. C. L. N. A. I. J. Koran, xvi. 38: "Some of them there were, whom Allah guided, and there were others doomed to err."

436.

Oh that great Allah would rebuild these skies,
And this sad earth, teeming with miseries:
　　And either rase my name from off his roll,
Or else relieve my dire necessities !

487.

Lord ! make Thy bounty's cup for me to flow,
And bread unbegged for day by day bestow:
　　Yea, with Thy wine make me beside myself,
No more to feel the headache of my woe !

488.

Ah, brand ! Ah, burning brand ! foredoomed
　　　　to burn
In dread Gehennom's furnace in thy turn !
　　Presume not to teach Allah clemency,
For who art thou to teach, or He to learn ?

---

486. N. This rather sins against Horace's canon
Nec Deus intersit," &c.
487. C. L. N A. I. J. Clearly a parody of Suh
phraseology

۴۸۶

یزدان خواهم جهان دگر گون کندی
واکنون کندی تا نگرم چون کندی
یا نامِ من از جریده بیرون کندی
یا روزیِ من ز غیب افزون کندی

۴۸۷

یا رب بکشای بر من از رزق دری
بی منّتِ مخلوق رسان ما حضری
از بادهٔ چنان مست نگهدار مرا
کز بیخبری نباشدم دردِ سری

۴۸۸

ای سوختهٔ سوختهٔ سوختنی
وی آتشِ دوزخ از تو افروختنی
تا کی گوئی که بر عُمَر رحمت کن
حق را تو کجا و رحمت آموختنی

---

488. C. L. N. A. I. J. I have availed myself of Fitz-
Gerald's and Keene's renderings. The story of Omar's
mother is an obvious afterthought.

489.

Cheer up ! your lot they settled yesterday !
Heedless of all that you might do or say,
　　Without so much as " By your leave " they
　　　　fixed
Your fate for all the morrows yesterday !

490.

I never would have come, had I been asked !
When would I choose to go, if I were asked ?
　　I would forswear this world, and would dis-
　　　　pense
With coming, being, going, were I asked !

491.

Man is a cup, his soul the wine therein ;
Flesh is a pipe, spirit the voice within.
　　O Khayyam, have you fathomed what man is ?
A magic lantern with a light therein !

---

489. C. L A B I. Predestination.
490. C. L. N. (in part) A. B. 1. J. So the Ecclesiast,
" Therefore I hated life, . . for all is vanity," &c. *Kai
shudami*, " When would I have gone ? "

۴۸۹

خوش باش که پخته اند سودای تو دی
ایمن شده از همه تمنّای تو دی
تو شاد بزی که بی تقاضای تو دی
دادند قرار کار فردای تو دی

۴۹۰

گر آمدنم بمن بُدی نامدمی
ور نیز شدن بمن بدی کی شدمی
به زان نبدی که اندر این عالم خاك
نه آمدمی نه شدمی نه بدمی

۴۹۱

آدم چو صراحی بود و روح چو می
قالب چو نی بود صدائی در وی
دانی چه بود آدم خاكی خیّام
فانوس خیالی و چراغی در وی

---

491   C. A I. Note *mé* (for *mai*) rhyming with *wé*.
Wé is Turanian (Bl, Prosody, xvii), and probably *mé*,
pronounced with the *Imála* (ibid, p v.), is the same.
Perhaps the Persian of Khorásán was affected by Turki.

492.

O skyey wheel! all base men you supply
With baths, mills, and canals that run not dry,
　　While good men have to pawn their goods
　　　　for bread :
Pray, who would give a fig for such a sky ?

493.

A potter at his work I chanced to see,
Pounding some earth and shreds of pottery ;
　　I looked with eyes of insight, and methought
'Twas Adam's dust with which he made so free !

494.

The henchman knows my *genus* thoroughly,
Likewise my *species* and *property* :
　　When *accidents* befall me he brings wine,
And that makes all the *difference* to me !

492.　B L

493　C L, A I J　Note the arrangement of the
prepositions *baz* . . . *baz*　Bl, Prosody, xʌii.

۴۹۲

ای چرخ همه خسیس را چیز دهی
گرمابه و آسیا و کاریز دهی
آزاده بنان شب گروگان بنهند
شاید که بَر اینچنین فلک تیز دهی

۴۹۳

بر کوزہگری بزیر کردم گذری
از خاک همی نمود هر دم تبری
من دیدم اگر ندید هر بی بصری
خاکِ پدرم بر کفِ هر کوزہگری

۴۹۴

چون جنس مرا خاصه بداند ساقی
صد فصل ز هر نوع براند ساقی
چون وا مانم برسمِ خود باده دهد
در حدِّ خودم درگذراند ساقی

---

494. C. L. A. I.   A play on terms of Logic. *Jins*,
genus: *Gamma* is transliterated by *Jim*, as in *Jalinus*, and
Adrijān for *trigōnon*, where the initial *A* is euphonic, as in
Astabal for *Stabulē*.

495.

Dame Fortune! all your acts and deeds confess
That you are foul Oppression's votaress.

　　You cherish bad men, and annoy the good;
Is this from dotage, or sheer foolishness?

496.

You, who in carnal lusts your time employ,
Wearing your precious spirit with annoy,

　　Know that these things you set your heart
　　　　upon
Sooner or later must the soul destroy!

497.

Hear from the spirit-world this mystery:
Creation is summed up, O man, in thee;

　　Angel and demon, man and beast art thou,
Yea, thou *art* all thou dost *appear* to be!

495.　C. L A. I. J　*Mu'takif*, a devotee
496.　L　Probably a gloss by some pious reader.

۴۹۵

ای دهر بکردهایِ خودِ معترفی
در خانقهِ جور و ستم معتکفی
نعمت بخسان دهی و زحمت بکسان
زین هردو برون نیست خری یا خرفی

۴۹۶

پیوسته ز بهرِ شهوتِ نفسانی
این جانِ شریف را همی رنجانی
آگاه نهء که آفت جان تو اند
انها که تو در آرزویِ ایشانی

۴۹۷

ای انکه خلاصهء چهار ارکانی
بشنو سخنی ز عالمِ روحانی
دیوی و ددی و مَلَکْ و انسانی
با تست هرانچه می نمائی آنی

---

497. L. Man, the microcosm. In line 2 for *sukhan az*
I read *sukhané zi*, to make the line scan.

498.

If popularity you would ensue,
Speak well of Moslem, Christian, and Jew ;
   So shall you be esteemed of great and small,
And none will venture to speak ill of you.

499.

O wheel of heaven, what have I done to you,
That you should thus oppress me ? Tell me true :
   To get a drink I have to cringe and stoop,
And for my bread you make me beg and sue.

500.

No longer hug your grief and vain despair,
But in this unjust world be just and fair ;
   And since the substance of the world is
     naught,
Deem yourself naught, and so shake off dull
     care !

---

498. L

499. L *Abrúy*, 'honour.' So Dante, *Par*, xvii 58,

۴۹۸

خواهی که پسندیدهٔ آذانم شوی
مقبول قبولِ خاصه و عام شوی
اندر پیِ مومن و جهود و ترسا
بد گوی مباش تا نکونام شوی

۴۹۹

ای چرخ چه کرده ام ترا راست بگوی
پیوسته فکندهٔ مرا در تگ و پوی
نانم ندهی تا نبری کوی بکوی
ابم ندهی تا نبری آب ز روی

۵۰۰

چندین غمِ بیهوده مخور شاد بزی
و اندر رهِ بیداد تو باداد بزی
چون آخرِ کار این جهان نیستی است
انگار که نیستی و آزاد بزی

"How salt the bread that others give, how hard the
climbing others' stairs."

500. L. B. In line 3 scan *nǐsătĭyast*.

501.

Each grain of dust that on the ground is shed
Was once a Venus brow or sunny head.

Blow the dust gently from thy cheek, fair
maid,
Twas once a curl whose owner now lies dead !

502.

Darvésh ! cast off that cloak of outward show ;
To outward show give not your life ; but go,

Don the old rug of *genuine* poverty,
And drum of empire beat that rug below !

503.

Lord ! I am tired of this low state of mine,
This wretched lot, this beggary of mine ;

Thou makest all from naught, bring me from
naught
Into that sacred being which is Thine !

---

501. From the *Firdaws ut-Tawáríkh*. Journal R A S.
vol. xxx, p. 356. Dr. Ross says it is attributed to Hakim
Sanái in the Haft Iqlim. Note the dotted *dáls*.

502 B. Abandon the outward form of sanctity, and
practise real self-abnegation, which is true sovereignty

٥٠١

هر ذرّه که در رویِ زمینی بوذست
خور شیذرخی زهره جببنی بوذست
گرد از رخِ نارنین بآزرم فشان
کان هم رخ و زلفِ نارنینی بوذست

٥٠٢

درویش ز تن جامهٔ صورت برکن
تا در ذههی بجامهٔ صورت تن
رو کهنه گلیمِ فقر بر دوش افکن
در زیرِ گلیم کوس سلطانی زن

٥٠٣

سیر آمذم ای خدای از پستئ خویش
از ذلك دلی و از تهی دستئ خویش
از نیست چو هست میکنی بیرون آر
زین نیستیم بحرمتِ هستئ خویش

" To beat a drum under a blanket " is an expression often
met with

503   Bring me from my phenomenal ' Not being" to
Thy absolute " Being" From the Firdaws ut-Tawáríkh
(Journal R. A. S., vol. xxx, p. 357), which states that this
was Omar's last utterance in verse.

Z

501.

Man cannot change what pen hath writ of yore;
Diet of sorrow breedeth heart-pang sore.

Spend thy whole life in shedding tears of blood,
Thou canst not add one teardrop to thy store.

505.

O heart! quit dalliance with the fragile ones,
Cease love-communion with the common ones;

Frequent the threshold of the pure Darvésh,
Thou may-t be chosen of the chosen ones.

506

O Shah! heaven portioned sovereignty to thee,
And saddled power thy glorious steed to be;

And where thy charger sets his golden hoofs
Earth glitters like some golden tapestry.

---

504   B.
505   B   *Ma lili*, " sickly, frail."   The *yá i tausífi* or
tauki before *charad*

٥٠۴

از رفته قلم هیچ دگر گون نشود

وزخوردن غم بجزجگر خون نشود

گر در همه عمر خویش خوناب، خوری

یك قطره از آن که هست افـزون نشود

٥٠٥

ای دل مطلب وصال معلولی چند

مشغول مشو بعشق مشغولی چند

پیرامن آستان درویشان گرد

باشد که شوی قبول مقبولی چند

٥٠٦

شاها فلکت بخسروی تعیـین کرد

وز بهر تو اسپ پادشاهی زین کرد

تا در حرکت سمند زرّین سم تو

بر گل ننهد پای زمین سیمین کرد

---

506. B. Possibly addressed to Malik Shah, and the
only panegyric ascribed to Omar. *Falakat*, the affixed
pronoun *Te* pertains to the verb.

507.

From heaven a spirit-whisper came to me,—
" Learn hence the force of the divine decree,—
    " Had I the power my circlings to control,
" Long since from giddiness I'd set me free."

508.

In this our round of coming and of going
Beginning and conclusion pass all knowing :
    No wight in all the world can tell us truly
Whence we have come and whither we are going '

—   —

507   B   *Rihāndama*, the past potential, " I might have
released "
    508   From the *Marsād ul 'Ibād* of Najmu-d-Din Abū
Bakri Rāzi, Journal R A S , xxx , 362   Note the archai

FINIS.

۵۰۷

در گوش دلم گفت فلك پنهانی

حکمی که قضا بود زمن می دانی

در گردش خویش اگر مرا دست بدی

خودرا برهاندمی ز سرگردانی

۵۰۸

در دایرهٔ کامدن و رفتن ماست

آنرا نه بدایت نه نهایت پیداست

کس می نزند دمی درین عالم راست

کین آمدن از کجا و رفتن بکجاست

forms, dotted *Dāls* and *baidā* for *paidā*. Compare Ecclesiastes iii. 21, revised version: "Who knoweth the spirit
of man, whether it goeth upward?"

تمام شد

خاتمة

خیّام بمن پدید آمد در خواب
گفتم شیخا ز تو مَنم در تب و تاب
جز محنت ازین نامه نمیدارم سود
گفتا که نکوئی کن و انداز در آب

تاریخ

حکیم خیّام در لندن خیمه ز نو همی زند

APPENDIX.

NOTE A.

On the Izáfat.

THE *Izáfat* is expressed by the short vowel *Kasra*, and this, like all short vowels, requires a consonant before it to carry it. Some grammarians, speaking loosely, say that the *Izáfat* is sometimes expressed by *Hamza* or *Yá*; what they mean is, *Hamza i maksura* or *Yá i maksura*, "*Kasra*-bearing *Hamza* or *Yá*."

When the *Izáfat* follows a word ending in silent *He*, as silent *He* is too weak to carry the *Izáfat*, *Hamza* is placed over the *He* to act as carrier of the *Izáfat* in its place (Of course *Hamza* is not wanted in the case of radical *He*, *e.g* in words like *Gáh* and *Sháh*, as radical *He* is itself a perfect consonant.)

When *Izáfat* follows a word ending in *Alif*, used as a letter of prolongation, euphonic *Yá* (as Vullers calls it) is inserted to carry the *Izáfat*. According to Mirza Ibrahim, *Hamza* is generally placed over this *Yá*. In Arabic words ending in *Alif* plus *Hamza* the *Hamza* itself carries the *Izáfat*, and no *Yá* is needed

After *Waw*, used as a letter of prolongation, euphonic *Yá* is usually inserted to carry the *Izáfat* following it, but occasionally the long *ú* is dissolved into short *ŭ* (*Zamma*) and *Waw*, and the *Waw* is thus set free to carry the *Izáfat* without the intervention of *Yá*. According to Mirza Ibrahim (Grammar, sect. 34), when *Yá* is used, *Hamza* is commonly placed over the *Yá*.

When the *Izáfat* follows a word ending in *Yá*, used as a letter of prolongation, Mirza Ibrahim says *Hamza* must be placed over the *Yá*, and this with the *Izáfat* carried by it is pronounced "*ye*." Other authorities, as Lumsden and Blochmann, say no *Hamza* is needed, but plain *Kasra* must be written under the *Yá* In this case the long final syllable is dissolved into its component letters, *viz* the short *i* (*Kasra*) and the letter of prolongation *Yá*, and the *Yá* is set free to carry the *Kasra* of the *Izáfat* following it Such dissolution of course leaves the medial *i* (*Kasra*) short, but it may be lengthened at will by putting a *tashdíd* over the *Yá*. I have followed the practice sanctioned by Lumsden and Blochmann

Mr. E. G. Browne (Journal R A S for 1895, p. 240), expresses the opinion that when *Yá* is used to carry the *Izáfat* after *Alif* or *Waw*, *Hamza* must not be super-added "To write *Yá* with *Hamza* is a pure archaism, never, so far as we know, found in MSS. written in Persia during the last four centuries, though maintained by Indian writers" He goes on to say that when the *Izáfat* follows words ending in *Yá*, used as a letter of prolongation, *Hamza* is generally written over the *Yá*. Both these propositions are controverted by high authorities, the former by some grammarians, including the native Persian grammarian Mirza Ibrahim, and the latter by Blochmann. Mr Browne holds the view that *Hamza* may only be used when there is a hiatus between two vowel-sounds; but, if so, how can we account for its use in such words as كوئى " thou said-t," which is pronounced *Gúyí*, and ماهئى " one fish," pronounced *Máhiyé*?

May not the explanation of these conflicting views be that pronunciation has varied and still varies? It seems probable that the old pronunciation of ساقئ من may have been *Sáqi 'i man*, and that consequently *Hamza* was written over the *Yá*, in other words was substituted for the *Yá*. (Lumsden, 1. pp. 19 and 29.) And this substitution of *Hamza* for *Yá* may, I think, still have continued after the pronunciation *Sáqi yi man* came into use.* Evidently this took place in cases in which one *Yá* follows another in a word, where the rule is to omit the dots under the first *Yá* and write *Hamza* over it, in other words to change *Yá* into *Hamza* (Lumsden, 1. 29), though the *Yá* is now pronounced as if it were plain *Yá*.

For these reasons, I think that the practice of writing *Hamza* over *Yá* in all these cases is legitimate

Hamza, being a consonant, can carry a short vowel like any other consonant. It is a guttural, but not so strong as *'ain*.

---

* The same remarks apply to hamzated *Yá* after *Alif* and *Wáw*, used as letters of prolongation.

NOTE B.

The Rubá'í

"By *Rubá'í* the Persians denote a short poem of a
certain metre and consisting of four hemistichs, *i e* of
two distichs, of which three hemistichs, viz, the first,
second, and fourth rhyme. Occasionally we find
Ruba'ís with four rhymes The Ruba'í, unlike the
Ghazal, is not restricted to a particular subject-matter.
In every good Ruba'í the fourth hemistich, or the
whole distich, is either elevated or witty and striking
or epigrammatical. The first three hemistichs merely
introduce the happy thought of the fourth. This is
elegantly expressed by the verse of Mirza Sáib 'The
last verse of a Ruba'í drives the nail through the heart;
the line above the lip is in my opinion better than the
eyebrow'—the two eyebrows being compared to the
two upper, and the two sides of the moustache to
the two lower hemistichs of a Ruba'í " (Blochmann's
Prosody, p 90)

Persian prosodians reckon no less than twenty-four
Ruba'í metres. But these are all reducible to two
radical forms, out of which all the rest proceed by
contraction, *tashín*, of two contiguous short syllables
into one long syllable * This will be seen at a glance
from the following table of each radical form.

---

* Moreover, lines ending in a single quiescent consonant are
reckoned to be in a different metre from those ending in two
quiescent consonants

Form 1.

$$- - \cup \, , \, \cup - - \cup \, , \, \cup - - \cup \, , \, \cup -$$

Form 2

$$- - \cup \, , \, \cup - \cup - \, , \, \cup - - \cup \, , \, \cup -$$

It will be observed that Form 1 is reducible by contraction into ten long syllables, while Form 2 cannot be reduced to less than eleven, nine long and two short. By ringing the changes on the various possible contractions, the so-called twenty-four metres are produced But all that the student need do, is to remember the two radical forms, and the fact that wherever two short syllables come together, they can be contracted into one long syllable. Blochmann warns students that the tables of ruba'i metres in Gladwin's ' Rhetoric, Prosody and Rhyme of the Persians " (Calcutta, 1801), in Forbes' Grammar, etc., are incorrect.

Attempts have frequently been made to reproduce the Ruba'i metre in English, but such attempts are doomed to failure. As a rule, admitting of few exceptions, foreign metres, like foreign idioms, are aliens which cannot be naturalized and this is certainly the case with the Ruba'i metres. Turn and twist the words as we may, it is impossible to make accents produce the effect of quantities, especially of a succession of long quantities, such as we meet with in most Ruba'i lines. Few translators have ventured to reproduce Horace's Sapphic and Alcaic odes in English verse in those metres, and this affords a strong presumption that the plan will not succeed with Persian. Bodenstedt, who himself had the faculty of writing very harmonious verse, told me that he was once commissioned to polish some of Hammer's essays in this style of versification, but found the task absolutely hopeless

Even if we could reproduce the metre (or scansion) correctly, we could not reproduce the rhythm, which is a different thing from the metre. Mr. C. S Calverley, in his paper on Metrical Translation (Works, p. 496), points out that English reproductions of classical metres almost always err in this respect. We cannot give the blend of metre and rhythm.

NOTE C.

Omar's Reform of the Calendar.

THE following account of this reform is given by Mahmud Shah Khulji in his commentary on the Zij i Ilkhani of Nasir ud Din Tusi. (See Sachau and Ethé, Catalogue of Bodleian MSS p. 930, No 1522.) The introduction to this commentary was published by John Greaves, London, 1652, and Hyde (Veterum Persarum Religio, p 209) has given the following passage from it .—

"Account of the era (*tarikh*) called the Era of Malik Shah. The philosophers in the time of Sultan Jalal ud Din Malikshah, son of Alp Arslan the Seljuk, determined

the era called after Sultan Jalal ud Din, wherein the
names of the months corresponded with the names of
the Persian months , but they described the latter as
'old style,' and named the new months 'Jalalian.'
And they reckoned the beginning of the year of this
era, namely the first of the Jalalian month Farvardin,
to be the day on the forenoon of which the sun reached
the point of the vernal equinox, that is, the real begin-
ing of spring. This was Friday, corresponding with
9th Ramazan 471 A H., and with 15th March of the
Alexandrian year 1390, and with 19th Farvardin (old
style) of the year 448 of the era of Yazhjird And
they made the eighteen days of Farvardin (O S), then
elapsed, intercalary days (*habisat*),* and hence the
commencement of the era is called the Malikshahian
intercalation. Some consider the months of this era to
be true solar months, *i.e.* periods wherein the sun by its
own motion passes through one sign. For instance,
Farvardin is the period in which the sun passes through
Aries, and so on. Thus the year commenced with the
true spring, and each three months made a true quarter.
But astronomers, in order to facilitate the construction
of almanacs, and the drawing up of tables, introduced
the practice of reckoning thirty days in each month
after the Persian fashion, in order that the number of
days on each page of an almanac might be equal And
they added the five extra days at the end of the month
Isfandarmoz. Hence the years of this era are true
solar years, and their length, according to the obser-

---

* *I e* the 19th Farvardin O S. became the 1st Farvardin N.S

vations on which this era is based, is 365 days, 14 minutes 32 seconds of a day, reckoning the day and night together as 60 minutes.* In other words, 365 days and a quarter of a day minus 28 seconds.† For this cause they added one intercalary day to every fourth or fifth year, whereby such year contained 366 days. When the intercalary day had been added to each fourth year seven or eight times it was added once to the fifth year"

In reading this account we must not confound the sign Aries with the constellation Aries. The Jalalian new year's day or nauroz was fixed at the first point of the sign Aries, which moves along with the vernal equinox, and not at the first point of the constellation Aries, which is stationary   In the time of Hipparchus (about 100 B C), the vernal equinox coincided with the entry of the sun into the constellation Aries, in other words, the sun's path on the Ecliptic crossed the celestial equator upwards on the very day on which the sun came into conjunction with the fixed star on the westernmost boundary of the constellation Aries. But in consequence of the precession of the equinoxes the vernal equinoctial point had been advanced more than halfway across the constellation Pisces by Omar's time.   Hence the " sign" Aries no longer corresponded

---

* According to Lockyer's "Elementary Astronomy," p. 210, the mean daily motion of the sun is only 59 minutes 8 seconds and a fraction

† Te seconds of an astronomical "hour ' or degree of right ascension.

with the constellation Aries. In modern astronomical parlance, the "sign" Aries means the thirty hours or degrees of right ascension (celestial longitude) counted from the vernal equinox. Omar clearly used the term in this modern sense, because the first point of his Aries coincided with the vernal equinox in his calendar, and because the length of his year agrees more nearly with that of the "solar" (or "tropical") year, which is measured from one equinox to the next, than it does with the longer "sidereal" year, which is measured from one conjunction of the sun with a fixed star to its next conjunction with such star.*

Khulji's idea that the months, containing as they do definite amounts of *mean* time, can exactly correspond with the times taken by the sun in passing through particular "signs" is of course a mistake. Owing to the inequality of the sun's apparent motions solar time is now before and now behind mean time, as may be seen from a sun-dial.

NOTE D.

Bibliography.

Mr. Heron Allen has kindly allowed me to use the following list of MSS. and lithographed copies of

---

* See Lockyer, p 220.

Omar's Ruba'iyat, given by him in his edition of the
Bodleian MS. I have made some additions which are
distinguished by brackets

MSS.

British Museum.

Original MSS, No 330, ff 109, containing 423
ruba'iyat (18th century).

Original MSS, No. 331, ff 92, containing 540 ruba'iyat
(A.H. 1033).

Additional MSS, No 27.261, containing a few
ruba'iyat in Section 15 (16th century)

Bodleian Library, Oxford.

MS, No. 524, containing 405 ruba'iyat
  „ No 525 [Written at Shiraz in 865 A H, No 140
  in the Ouseley collection, referred to by me as B]
  „ No 1210. A collection of Miscellaneous Poems,
  containing several ruba'iyat on pp. 88-90.

Cambridge University Library

MS., Add 1055, ff 222, containing 801 ruba'iyat. Not
dated, but its first owner inscribed his name in it
in A H 1195. [Brought by Mr. Whitley Stokes
from Madras.]

India Office.

MS, No. 2420, ff 212-267, containing 512 ruba'iyat
  [Referred to as I in my notes]
  „ No. 2486, ff 158-194, containing 362 ruba'iyat
  [Referred to by me as J]

Bengal Asiatic Society's Library, Calcutta.

MS., No. 1548, containing 516 ruba'iyat. [Referred to by me as A]

Bibliothèque Nationale, Paris.

MS., Supplément Persan 745. A Dīwān of Emad dated A H. 786. One of the owners of this has written 6 ruba'iyat of Omar upon the blank side of fol 64, in a handwriting of the end of the 9th or beginning of the 10th century A H.

Ancien Fonds 349, ff. 181-210, 213 ruba'iyat, dated A.H. 920.

Supplément Persan 823, ff. 92-113, 349 ruba'iyat, dated A.H. 934.

Supplément Persan 826, ff. 391-394, 75 ruba'iyat, dated A.H. 937.

Supplément Persan 793, f. 104, 6 ruba'iyat in an 11th century (A H.) handwriting.

Konigliche Bibliothek, Berlin.

MS., No. 35, containing 238 ruba'iyat.
„	No. 666,	„	65	„
„	No. 672,	„	40	„
„	No. 674,	„	380	„
„	No. 697,	„	43	„

Herzogliche Bibliothek, Gotha.

A MS. and a Turkish version by Daulat Shah.

Khuda Bakhsh Library, Bankipur (Patna).

MS. dated A.H. 961-2, and containing 603 ruba'iyat.

[Sprenger mentions a MS of Omar containing 34 pp. of
24 bayts, in the Topkhana Library at Lucknow.
(Now lost.)

Mr. Beveridge found in the Mullá Firúz Library at
Bombay a MS (No 78 of printed catalogue) which
he thinks of little value. (Journal R A S,
vol. xxxiii., p. 70.)

The Bengal Asiatic Society, I believe, bought Blochmann's MS. of Omar, containing over 500 quatrains,
but Mr. Beveridge does not mention having seen
it there.

In the Library of All Souls' College, Oxford, there is a
MS. containing about 200 quatrains, probably of
17th century A D

The Munich Library has no copy of Omar.

In his "Redekunste Persiens," Hammer mentions a
MS. of Omar containing 300 quatrains, which is
probably now at Vienna.]

LITHOGRAPHS.

Teheran, 1861, containing 460 ruba'iyat.
Tabriz, 1868,   „   453   „
Lucknow, 1868,   „   716   „
       „ 1878,   „   763   „   [Referred to
       by me as L.]
Other Lucknow editions were issued in 1882 and 1883.
Lucknow,   1894, containing 770 ruba'iyat
St. Petersburg, 1888,   „   453   „   [See Ethé.
       "Neu-Persische Litteratur," Sect 32.]

A selection of poems published at Teheran, 1857, containing 230 ruba'iyat of Omar, and other ruba'iyat of Baba Tahri, Abū Sa'id, Attar, &c.

A similar collection lithographed at Bombay, in A.H. 1297, containing 756 ruba'iyat attributed to Omar.

[Whalley's lithograph (Muradabad, about 1874), containing 87 quatrains

Mr. Heron Allen also mentions the *Atash Kadah*, which contains 31 quatrains.

And many other *Tazkiras* might be cited.]

PRINTED TEXTS.

Calcutta, 1252 A.H., containing 492 ruba'iyat. [Referred to by me as C.]

Nicolas, Paris, 1867, containing 464 ruba'iyat. [Referred to by me as N.]

Whinfield, London, 1883, containing 500 ruba'iyat.

[Heron Allen, 1898, „ 158 „ from the Bodleian MS.]

ADDITIONS AND CORRECTIONS.

Introduction, p. xx. The statement in the text must be qualified. Two more MSS. of the 10th century A.H have been brought to light by Mr. Heron Allen, one at Paris containing 349, and one at Bankipur containing 516 quatrains.

Introduction, p. xxvi., &c. *For* Fitz-Gerald *read* FitzGerald.

Page 2, note. In modern Persian books, *e g.* Q and T , the *Ya* in *Rubá iyát* bears *tashdíd*, but in the Bodleian MS. it is omitted.

Quatrain 42 is ascribed by AK. to Afzul Kashi (d 707 A.H.).

Quatrain 93 is ascribed by T. to Pír Ansári (d. 481 A H)

Quatrain 108 In line 1, for *Súr* B. reads *'adn*, after Koran, ix 73, where Sale notes that *'adn* does not mean "Eden" in the Hebrew sense, but "a garden of permanent occupation."

Quatrain 143, note. *Al-Shaitán fi-l Haiámain*, Blochmann, *Ain i Akbari* (translation), 293, note 3.

Quatrain 178, note. For *khuiad* read *khurad* "blackness."

Quatrain 198   Hemp (*Hashish* or *Ganja*) is invoked by Hafiz in Ode 282 (Brockhaus) as "Parrot discoursing of mysteries"   Browne's "Year amongst the Persians," p. 551.

Quatrain 228 is quoted in the *Dabistān* (Shea & Troyer, iii 150) as expressing the Sufi view as to the future state   When the rational soul has become degraded to the level of the animal or the vegetive soul, men will rise as animals or even mere plants   Contrariwise, when the man has "moved upward working out the beast," he will rise as an angel soul   Thus the *Masnavi*, p. 159 .

> I died as mineral and arose a plant ;
> I died as a plant and rose again an animal ,
> I died as an animal and arose a man.
> Why then should I fear to become less by dying ?
> I shall die once again, as a man,
> To rise an angel perfect from head to foot.
> Again, when I suffer dissolution as an angel,
> I shall become what passes the conception of man.
> Let me then become non-existent, for non existence
> Sings to me in organ tones, " To Him shall we return "

Of course, this does not mean that the souls of men transmigrate into those of animals or angels, for the Sufis reject transmigration as "false and vain." (*Gulshan i Rāz*, l. 106)   What is meant is that the soul of the good man is evolved into a higher soul, while the soul of the bad man retrogrades to one of its inferior constituents, viz the animal or the vegetive soul   See *Gulshan i Rāz*, p. 33.

Quatrain 236 was first explained by Mr. C E. Wilson in the *Academy*, October, 1883.

Quatrain 369. Cp. Dugald Stewart, "Active and Moral Powers" (Works, vii., p 34)

"These lines of Pope have been censured by some writers as savouring of Spinozism. I suspect that the authors of this criticism have been but slightly acquainted with Spinoza's writings, otherwise they would never have confounded a system which goes to the complete annihilation of every religious sentiment with a doctrine which, although somewhat approaching it in phraseology, originated in feelings of deep if not mystical devotion. The former explains away the existence of God by identifying him with matter, the latter gives life and expression to matter by representing every object as full of God."

Mark Pattison adds : " Pope doubtless meant in these lines to express the omnipresence of the Supreme Mind, Creator and Preserver of the universe. Cardinal Bellarmine says, 'To become the soul of the world there is no necessity for God to be of one and the same substance with the world ; God is absolutely in everything, there cannot possibly be anything where God is not.' An imaginative mind in daily contact with the life of nature, ever varying yet ever one, is necessarily thrown into this train of sentiment."— Pattison's " Pope's Essay on Man," p 88.

Quatrain 423. *For* "Thou wentest and" *read* "Lo ! thou."

Appendix, p. 353 The Bengal Asiatic Society's MS is missing I used Professor Cowell's copy of it

Ingram Content Group UK Ltd.
Milton Keynes UK
UKHW021117180423
420361UK00006B/579